ENCOUNTER
WITH
SILENCE

Reflections from
the Quaker Tradition

John Punshon

Friends United Press
Richmond, Indiana

Quaker Home Service • London

Copyright ©1987 by John Punshon

Printed in the United States of America
Published by
Friends United Press
101 Quaker Hill Drive
Richmond, IN 47374
And
Quaker Home Service
London, England

Library of Congress Cataloging-in-Publication Data

Punshon, John, 1935
Encounter with Silence

1.   Public Worship—Society of Friends 2. Spiritual life—Quaker authors
3.   Punshon, John, 1935—Religion 4. Society of Friends—Doctrines. I. Title.
BX7737.P86   1987   264'.096 87-181
ISBN 0-913408-96-4
ISBN 0-85245-201-2 (Quaker Home Service)

Copyright 1987 John Punshon
Published 1987 by Friends United Press, Richmond, Indiana
And Quaker Home Service, London, England.
Second Printing 1989
Third Printing 1994
Fourth Printing 1996
Fifth Printing 1998
Sixth Printing 2000

ENCOUNTER WITH SILENCE

Contents

FOREWORD

Reading this serious and moving contemporary story of a soul, I was reminded of several encounters I have had with Quakerism over the years. The first—and perhaps most lasting—was the day about eleven years ago when I was invited to lecture in a Quaker meetinghouse in Oak Park, Illinois. I was working heavily on Meister Echkart at that time in my life, and I still had not published or even preached anything about him publicly. I decided that my 'coming out' as an Eckhartphile would happen on Quaker soil. Thus, I spoke on some twenty-one themes that I found of deep interest to myself and others interested in a spirituality of justice-making as found in Meister Eckhart. The moment I finished my presentation—from a rocking chair, I recall (it was the first and last time anyone has offered me a rocking chair to lecture from)—a strong and vibrant woman spoke with great authority from the back of the room: "My God, it sounds *exactly* like George Fox." It was the voice of the woman who ran things at that Quaker house. I also remember visiting the Quaker house in Paris when I accompanied a delegation of Catholics against the Vietnam War in a visit we made to the various negotiating parties in Paris in 1971. These twin experiences of shared mysticism and shared prophetic concern have long drawn me to respect the charism and the historical accomplishments of resistance bound up in a grounded mysticism that I find in the Quaker tradition. "Picket and pray" one person has called that tradition.

This dialectic of mysticism and prophecy names my spiritual quest as an adult since I first went to Paris in 1967 to study spirituality on the advice of Thomas Merton. (Presumably I had been attempting to *live* some during the nine years of spiritual and intellectual training that preceded my intellectual quest. I was reminded in reading John Punshon's book on several occasions of the hour a day of meditation, for example, that was part of our discipline as Dominicans–a rich time of silence indeed.) But in 1967 with the Vietnam War raging and the civil rights movement inspiring so many, I went with really one question on my mind: What is the relation between prayer and politics? Between mysticism and prophecy? Between space and time? Between Christ and Jesus? Each of my writings since has been an attempt to formulate some kind of workable answer to these longings. John Punshon's book contributes significantly to the questions behind these questions and to the answers to them. I will speak to just a few of the contributions he makes in this very readable, very honest, and well thought out book.

Wisely, John Punshon centers his reflections around that central Quaker (and mystical) theme, silence. Meister Eckhart* (1260-1329) says: "Nothing in all creation is so like God as silence." And, again: "The most beautiful thing which a person can say about God would be for that person to remain silent from the wisdom of an inner wealth. So, be silent and quit flapping your gums about God." It is in silence that the Spirit of God, the source of all creation and revelation, is allowed to bubble up from its "underground river" (another of Eckhart's images) into our psyches and from there, hopefully, into our culture and its institutions or into new expressions of faith and living. In the tradition of Eckhart, Teresa, Francis of Assisi and others whom he quotes, John Punshon lays out the many lessons to be learned from being with being, and therefore from being silent. I especially appreciate his observation that silence "disarms the sentimental feelings and habits of mind which arise from self-centeredness" (p. 61). Sentimentalism appears to be the raging religion of the West in the last days of colonial empire-building. John Punshon, like mystics before him, senses that true prophetic action must come not just from rage or dissatisfaction or from alternative political ideology, but from deep within: From an inner silence whence all creativity comes.

I appreciate very much John Punshon's sense of history and of the continuity he sees between Quaker contemplation and that of monasticism before Quakerism. With this sense of shared appreciation of mysticism he is well equipped to take on the bigger ecumenical questions of our day as he does when he talks of the wisdom learned from the Muslim woman: How does the Christian tradition relate to the other world faiths? In a post-colonial period, that becomes a major issue if world peace and justice are ever to happen. I believe this book opens an important avenue in the right direction, for it is saying that there will be no world ecumenism without the mystical dimensions being practiced and recovered in the West. I agree wholeheartedly with that prognosis, and that is one more reason why the Quaker tradition of mystical prayer for everyone—that "this revelation comes direct to every single human being, without exception," as the author puts it (p. 181)—is basic to such a global spiritual awakening.

Quakerism, John Punshon assures us, has "always seen this process of revelation as taking place continually and personally. Revelation comes to individuals, and they act upon it....Their actions become a part of history" (p. 182). Again, I am reminded of Eckhart's same sense of the work of God taking place in the depths of us all: "In the depths of our being, where justice and work are one, we work one work and a New Creation with God." God's work and, therefore, revelation has never ceased, according to Eckhart: "God forever creates and forever begins to create, and creatures are always being created and in the process of beginning to be created."

John Punshon wisely criticizes a theology which he calls "subtly anti-prophetic" for its locking Divinity up in an "intellectual ghetto" between "the covers of a black book" (p. 184). An anti-prophetic bias is also an anti-mystical bias which rationalism and religion's flight from its own mystical traditions have spawned. Once again, Eckhart spoke to this same concern when he said that "every creature is a word of God and a book about God." That is why silence is so powerful. It allows us to sit in the awesome presence of the mystery of God's creation and our place in it and with all God's creation. Out of this shared silence new birth is not only possible but natural and necessary. The word of God is not limited to the educated ones, the privileged ones, the literate ones—or to the two-legged ones. Creation itself, ongoing as it is, and open to breakthrough in nature and in the human psyche (which is also nature), is a fullsome source of revelation.

The living out of the living word of God goes on in history and in matter, and deep questions are raised by any effort to excite the "divine light" in persons today. Eckhart spoke of the *'ancilla animae,'* the 'spark of the soul' that all of us share in common. To critique the fires we start (and the ones we resist starting) is basic to our divine task of creating. Can Christianity, for example, afford to confuse itself and others by offering so many multiple interpretations of itself as is currently the case? Or might we find a common root in the direction toward which John Punshon points: That of a theology of the Holy Spirit that derives from mystical experience and leads to prophetic action? If so, then all those groups that call themselves Christian may find themselves regrouping and re-creating from their shared wisdom and from their shared limits.

If I were to criticize this book as to the shared limits of Quakerism as presented herein, I would cite only one disappointment: That is that I find chapter thirteen to be weak as to Incarnation, as to the role of spirit in matter, in our flesh, in our eating and drinking of the Cosmic Christ of the universe. In short, the real power of the Eucharist is far too daintily dealt with. It is seen in far too anthropocentric and too non-cosmological a context. (One can hardly fault John Punshon for this, since ninety-nine percent of the theologians professing to write from a belief in the Eucharist are at least as anthropocentric.) Yet something of great importance is being said here: *we Christians do not yet know what it is we are outgrowing or what it is we are renewing or even giving birth to or the extent to which the living tradition of the historical and prophetic Jesus has yet to be linked to the mystical tradition of the Cosmic Christ.* Perhaps when that day comes—as come it must very soon in our lifetimes—Quakers will find themselves more fully a part of that history which, in John Punshon's words, "cultivated the Quaker values long before there were any Quakers" (p. 97). That history will find itself more bent on the essence of the Gospels, which surely has everything to do with silence and prophetic witness in a post-Constantinian way of following the pre-Constantinian Jesus. When that day comes our dualisms will cease, and we will see in our rich diversity a treasure ready-made for creating the reign of God with more imagination and spirit and effectiveness than history records we have done up to now. Our dualisms and differences will melt into a dialectic and creative tension, a "reconciliation of opposites" and a deep appreciation of the depths we share in common: specifically, a living mysticism that celebrates our shared existence and a lived-out prophecy that guarantees the right to beauty of generations of earth dwellers destined to follow us.

Matthew Fox

*All references to Eckhart may be found in Matthew Fox, *Meditations with Mesiter Eckhart* (Santa Fe: Bear & Co., 1982). For a more complete exposure to Eckhart see Matthew Fox, *Breakthrough: Meister Eckhart's Creation Spirituality in New Translation* (New York: Doubleday, 1980). Matthew Fox is currently director of the Institute in Culture and Creation Spirituality at Holy Names College, Oakland, California.

Introduction

The Religious Society of Friends grew up in England and America three centuries ago. Since that time there has been a vigorous and independent Quaker tradition in each country. Nowadays Friends are found all around the world and are no longer distinguished by their plain speech, their distinctive grey clothing, their wealth or their Anglo-Saxon origins.

In the last century, two distinct forms of Quakerism have emerged, based largely on different patterns of worship. Many Friends now come together in programmed meetings where, under the guidance of a pastor, they sing hymns, listen to Bible readings and a sermon, and pause for a little while for 'open worship'. This is a period of silent devotion at the heart of the meeting where any member of the congregation may offer prayer or give a spoken message.

Though the programmed meetings are the newer tradition among Friends, their members form a distinct majority of the Society. The period of open worship is one of the many things they have in common with other Quakers whose meetings are not programmed. These Friends of the older tradition meet for what is usually an hour of silent prayer and meditation punctuated only by short spoken messages. Newcomers to each tradition are often astonished to discover the existence of the other kind of Friend.

This account of my own experience of unprogrammed worship

is an attempt to explain the depth and strength of the roots that nourish both traditions. It is a personal view, and in no sense authoritative, for authorities are something Friends, by and large, manage to do without.

Additionally, I have tried to relate the Quaker experience to the much older tradition of contemplative prayer which the church has nourished since early times. In our day we are witnessing a revival of interest in the spiritual life which is transforming the lives of individuals in all branches of the church and cutting across denominational boundaries. I hope also that what I have to say may contribute to that process.

I would like to express my thanks to all those Friends who have helped me with this book by letting me argue with them. Among this number I would like to mention particularly Kara Cole of the one tradition, and Sandra Cronk of the other, two women ministers the Society is blessed to have. They did not always agree with me, so I have to state that the opinions given here are mine alone. I would also like to thank my Friend John Noon for reading the manuscript, and my indefatigable editor, Barbara Mays, of Friends United Press.

John Punshon
Birmingham, England
15 September 1986

Silence
in the
Quaker
Tradition

Stillness
and
Speaking

When I began this account of Quaker worship as I have come to experience it, I wanted a text which would sum up all I have to say. Ranging the length and depth of the Bible, I considered and rejected many words. Ultimately I came to see what I know of the Quaker experience to be summed up in the words of Hebrews 4:12, "For the word of God is living and active, sharper than any two-edged sword, piercing to the division of soul and spirit, of joints and marrow, and discerning the thoughts and intentions of the heart." I chose this verse because it expresses both a challenge and a power. I have known both, sitting in the silence of unprogrammed Friends meetings, and they have given meaning to my life.

Though there are no reports of speaking in tongues in the early Quaker meetings, it is pretty clear that there was an immense power to be felt there. The Greek word 'ecstasy' literally means being turned inside out, and the written records indicate that this is the sort of feeling many of the first Friends had as the sword of the Holy Spirit searched their hearts. This experience shaped the life of their community and inspired their worship when they came together. It is the clue to the origins of both the Quaker lifestyle and the unprogrammed meeting for worship.

An English Friend, Charles Marshall of Bristol, describes the response of a meeting he was in to the preaching of a travelling

Quaker minister in 1654. "(he) lifted up his voice as a trumpet and said, 'I proclaim spiritual war with the inhabitants of the earth, who are in the fall and separation from God, and prophesy to the four winds of heaven.' And these words dropped among the seed, and so went on in the mighty power of God almighty..."

Marshall reports the "seizings of souls and prickings at heart which attended that season; some fell upon the ground, others crying out under the sense of opening their states, which indeed gave experimental knowledge of what is recorded, Acts 2:37." He continues, "Indeed it was a notable day, worthy to be left on record, that our children may read, and tell to their children, and theirs to another generation, that the worthy noble acts of the arm of God's salvation may be remembered, which have been the way of the Lord, leading his servants through generations, etc."

A year or two earlier, the founder of the Society of Friends, George Fox, visited Westmorland. Another of the earliest Quakers, Francis Howgill, describes how his preaching "reached unto all our consciences and entered into the inmost part of our hearts, which drove us to a narrow search and to a diligent inquisition concerning our state, through the Light of Christ Jesus." He continues with a description of the meeting, "...and, as we waited upon him in pure silence, our minds out of all things, his heavenly presence appeared in our assemblies, when there was no language, tongue, nor speech from any creature."

There then follow his most famous words: "The Kingdom of Heaven did gather us and catch us all, as in a net, and his heavenly power at one time drew many hundreds to land..." As in Charles Marshall's account, there is a hint of the judgment here, and Howgill concludes appropriately with a reflection on the importance of what has happened. "O blessed day! the memorial of which can never pass out of my mind. And thus the Lord, in short, did form us to be a people for his praise in our generation."

Though brief, these passages are like title deeds to a property. They show all the salient features of the Quaker understanding of gospel ministry and the inheritance into which its hearers may enter. The preachers, John Camm and George Fox, speak prophetically—under divine inspiration rather than as interpreters of a written revelation. Their words are sown like seeds in the souls of their hearers, who wait silently for God to bring forth fruit from them. One challenges, the other consoles.

Such is the hearers' experience of divine power that only the highest words in the Christian vocabulary will do it justice. Salvation comes upon them. They are gathered into the kingdom of heaven. They have a sense of being the Lord's people.

We are separated by over three centuries from those times. The Society of Friends has survived and developed a rich heritage of social action and personal religious experience. Its characteristic form of unprogrammed worship has roots in history but also a continuing vitality. Worshipping in silence is part of a particular way of being called by God, and as such, still influences the practice of all parts of the Society of Friends, including those where it is now the custom to meet, and sing hymns, listen to the reading of the scriptures, and hear sermons.

I suppose also that this is why it is really inappropriate in modern times to talk about 'silent' meetings, for the spoken ministry, except on some occasions, is an integral part of the silence, not an interruption of it. In the first letter of Peter, we read, "As each has received a gift, employ it for one another, as good stewards of God's varied grace; whoever speaks, as one who utters oracles of God..." This has always been Friends' way. Ministry is seen as the exercise of one of the gifts of the Spirit, which cannot be regulated or formalised, these gifts being given, withheld and withdrawn in a way that defies human reasoning. Friends do not believe they are ever given once and for all, or that anybody can be ordained to possess them.

Robert Barclay, the great defender of Quakerism in its second generation, wrote in his *Apology* (1676), "But in the true church of Christ...the Spirit of God is the orderer, ruler and governor; as in each particular, so in the general." His emphasis still remains that of the Society. Though the programmed tradition calls pastors to serve its meetings, it joins the unprogrammed tradition in endorsing Barclay's assertion, "...it is left to the free gift of God to choose any whom he seeth meet thereunto, whether rich or poor, servant or master, young or old, yea, male or female. And such as have this call verify the gospel, by preaching not in speech only, but also in power and in the Holy Ghost..."

It took me many years before I came to the conclusion that these things were not just rationalisations of the Quakers' peculiar position, but the essence of Christianity. It did, and does, frighten me. The reason for my fear is that I now cannot hide in the anonymity of silence. I am required to be attentive to God in case I am called upon to speak. I must uphold the meeting in prayer. I must accept my priesthood, and the only sacrifice I have to make is myself. In a word, at meeting I encounter the holy. I know from experience that the priesthood is the vocation of all believers, and I am not at liberty to relinquish it.

In a letter to one of his relatives, the early Friend Isaac Penington explains why this is:

> This gospel, through the great mercy of God, I have at length heard preached; and I have not heard MAN, but the voice of my Beloved; whose voice is welcome to me, though in the meanest boy or most contemptible female. For, in Christ, there is neither male nor female; nor should his Spirit, which is not limited to male, be quenched in any. And though thou, through prejudice, call this speaking of the Spirit through servants and handmaids PRATING, yet the Lord can forgive thee; for surely, if thou knew what thou didst herein, thou wouldst not thus offend the Lord;—extolling preaching by man's wisdom, from a minister made by man, for gospel-preaching, and condemning the preaching of persons sent by God, in the immediate inspiration of his Spirit. I am confident, if, without prejudice, and in the fear of God, thou didst once hear such, thou wouldst not be able to forbear saying in thy heart, It is the voice of God, of a truth:—but, that which hath not the sheep's ear can never own the voice of the true shepherd. (*Letters of Isaac Penington,* p. 220.)

These accounts of traditional Quaker spirituality, and others like them, give some interesting perspectives on the practice of unprogrammed meetings. Many people think the most important thing about such meetings nowadays is that they are held in silence, with no premeditated words or song. The silence is certainly essential, but, by itself, it is not enough to constitute a Quaker meeting. What goes on in the silence is far more important.

It is stillness, I am sure, not the absence of noise, which is the sign of true Friends worship. Stillness is a personal quality, not something in the environment. During the war in Vietnam there was a Friends meeting in Saigon at which worship was offered to the sound of gunfire, and on occasion while the city was under bombardment. It is hard to think of less silent circumstances than those.

The inward stillness which can find God in such a situation is not that of the soul seeking a quiet hour for meditation or reflection.

Nor can it come from a mind whose ultimate values are in the world. It is in the stillness that the challenge of the Holy Spirit comes. I know that my own mind and attention are often somewhere else when I am at worship—in the past, or perhaps the future. Nevertheless, I have to overcome these things. I have to still my mind. I have to direct the flow of my attention inward. It is to this that I am called.

St. Teresa of Avila speaks of what she calls the prayer of recollection, "...for you must understand that this is not altogether a supernatural thing, but is quite within our own power, and we can do it whenever we choose; I mean, of course, with God's help, for without this we can do nothing at all, not so much as have a single good thought. For you must observe that this recollection is not a suspension of the powers of the soul, but only a shutting them up, as it were, within ourselves."

I found great comfort in discovering Teresa, whom I have come to admire and recognise as a great personal inspiration. Here, I believe her to be describing a practise similar in most points to what I know in the stillness of a Friends meeting. It is a state of great attentiveness, not of abandon. It involves an awareness of one's being, not one's doing. That is why it is still. Silence is defined from outside, stillness from within.

The stillness of meeting was beautifully described by George Keith in 1670, though in a rather convoluted sentence:

> ...they became greatly endeared towards one another, in all pureness and tenderness of love, and finding the great benefit and advantage which they had in one anothers company, presence and fellowship, as of one being a strength to another, their life and spirit reaching unto them oft without all words, yea in the silence or ceasing of all words they were drawn to meet often together, for that in the presence and company of one another they were inwardly refreshed, comforted, quickened and strengthened, through that communion and communication of the spirit and life of God, from vessel to vessel, as from one upon all, and from all upon one, and this is that communion of saints which is a mystery forever... (*The Benefit, Advantage, and Glory of Silent Meetings*, 1670, p. 10)

The spiritual path which I have sought to follow since I met the divine reality, (long after I became a nominal Quaker), has led me into this experience of stillness, which I seek to realise in meeting for worship. Like Teresa, I know it is attainable. But I also know that when Friends practise it together, there is a great release of God's power into their worship and their lives.

Though the cultivation of silence as a religious practise was a part of the monastic life in the Middle Ages, the reason for its use was primarily personal. It was an aid to the interior life. At the Reformation, however, it seems to have acquired a new use. At that time many people were experimenting with new forms of worship as a consequence of the doctrinal battles in which they were engaged. There is evidence that in some places, in the Netherlands and England in particular, the practise was adopted of congregations giving up the traditional forms of worship and waiting together in silence.

Why they should have done so is now a matter shrouded in mystery. These groups were never large, and reports of their existence are infrequent. Nevertheless, enough is known of the circumstances in which they appeared to make it likely that the silence they practised had two purposes. It was the natural medium of prayer. That much came down from the Middle Ages. But more important than that was its novelty when practised as a sign of the unity, loyalty and confession of a group, defining itself as a part of the kingdom of heaven by a truculent rejection of what it saw as the forms to which corrupt or wordly Christianity conformed. This is also a part of the origins of Quaker silence.

There are historical precedents for Quaker ministry too. Speaking out of the silence is a curious hybrid activity which does not quite fit any of the usual categories of preaching, teaching or testifying in church. It was obviously perfectly familiar to the early Quakers, who were rumbustious to a fault. They had far more in common with the troopers in Cromwell's regiments of cavalry than they did with the refined, English Catholic expatriates who were to be found among the Carmelites and Trappists of continental Europe. That cannot be said for all of their successors.

One of the Puritan practises with which they were familiar, and which had been suppressed by the authorities under Queen Elizabeth I, was that of 'prophesying'. This was a form of mutual religious education which began as a sort of class meeting in which ministers and lay people came together to study the scriptures and arrive at commonly accepted interpretations of what they meant. It seems that what happened there approximated to the sort of utterances later familiar in Quaker meetings. The meaning of the text was held forth in the Spirit, and the church itself came thereby into a common understanding.

Though these practises were not widespread, they are nevertheless part of the spirit of Puritanism and could flourish only where people believed that the church was a society of equals. Quakerism has significant roots in the Puritan tradition, and this is why it was so easy for one branch of the Society of Friends in modern times to call pastors to serve its meetings. Puritan pastors where called by their congregations and not assigned to them by some higher authority. They certainly had a leadership role (not absent from early Quakerism, incidentally), but it was discharged with the assistance, and under the guidance, of ordinary lay members of the church community. The minister was properly regarded as a layman carrying out certain specialist tasks. This remains one of the essentials of Quakerism in both its programmed and unprogrammed varieties.

Another feature of Quakerism which comes from its Reformation origins is a suspicion of, or hostility towards, the outward expression of religion in ritual, dogma and hierarchy. This is partly due to a streak of what could be called 'critical reasonableness' which is to be found in most Quakers. Its deeper root links Friends indissolubly with their other spiritual grandparents, the churches of the Anabaptist tradition. In that quarter there is a collective memory of having been on the wrong end of persecution for religion's sake. It also carries with it a suspicion of the power of the state, for Quakerism grew out of that wing of the Reformation which was as opposed to state-sanctioned Protestantism as it was to the older Catholic faith.

The practise of Quaker worship has a strength which goes far beyond the simple act of sitting in an unprogrammed meeting. It defines a community of believers and the way they understand the bond that exists between them. It gives expression to their sense of the indescribable holiness of God. This has probably never been better put than by Paul in his first letter to the Corinthians: "...we teach what scripture calls: 'the things that no eye has seen and no ear has heard, things beyond the mind of man, all that God has prepared for those that love him.' These are the very things that God has revealed to us through the Spirit, for the Spirit reaches the depths of everything, even the depths of God."

The
Cross
and the
Light

The meeting for worship, offering in turn silence, stillness and an encounter with divine grace, dovetails neatly into traditional Quaker spirituality. Preferring to see the religious life in terms of personal experience rather than theological formulations, early Friends heard a deep echo of what had happened to them in Paul's words about the Holy Spirit searching the depths of all things, even the depths of God. They knew this transforming power, and they knew that as they gathered in worship, they had the experience of being 'searched'.

There is nothing mysterious about this. When I go to meeting with the intention of worshipping God, I have serious preparations to make. I understand Jesus to be saying that if I truly desire to follow him and to enter the kingdom of heaven, I must be willing to open my heart completely, give everything I have and hold nothing back in my own secret places. I must, in a word, be willing to be searched myself. I must bring all those things that make me the person I am, good and bad, acceptable and unacceptable, and place them before God. I must, to use a special Quaker phrase, 'come to the light'.

There are two dimensions to this process. In one sense, I have to bring my life to the light whenever I go to meeting. Even if I fail, I must make the effort at self-surrender, for my life is lived from day to day. On the other hand, a lasting offering of myself to God needs time, for it must have deep roots in personal faith, and such roots grow neither quickly nor easily. So meeting involves me in the encounter with God at two levels. On any given occasion I will be seeking communion and offering up myself in God's service. But over time, and in my continuing daily life, God will be preparing me and forming me for that same service.

Hence the distinction between silence and stillness. Silence is simply a preparation for being still, the means of worship, not the worship itself. Prayers, praises, preaching and spiritual song arose in the hearts of the early Friends as and when they felt the Spirit move in the silence. They were able to discern the Spirit because of the stillness of their hearts, not because their bodies were motionless.

Nor was the stillness a special technique for worship invented by the Quakers. It is simply the awareness of God's presence which so many people of faith carry with them all the time, and which enables them gracefully to rise above the distractions of everyday life. Stillness is intensified in moments of private prayer and communion, and enhanced when experienced in the company of others. This is why Friends need to meet for worship. The practice of stillness needs guidance and nourishment, for we are not self-sufficient. Just as there is a Trappist way of stillness, there is a Quaker way, and the meeting for worship crowns it.

When I go to meeting, therefore, I do not expect something that is different in kind from my ordinary, workaday experiences of God. What happens in the silence is an extension of my personal spiritual life, and a fulfillment of it. As I have grown in grace over the years, I have come to see how the long-term pattern of my life has been changed and shaped by the discipline of waiting. I made a commitment to God early in life, as I shall explain, but my true conversion of heart came much later, and it was through my experience of unprogrammed worship that God prepared me for it.

After I had been attending meeting for a while without much clarity as to why I went, I realised that if what I was looking for was religious thrills every time, I was going to be disappointed. I felt deep communion at points during the meeting, I felt deeply satisfied afterwards, but those moments did not come at my command or expectation. They were given to me periodically to punctuate what was otherwise the not noticeably religious experience of sitting there as unobtrusively as possible with not much going on. What I had to do was simply to wait and exercise patience. That was the discipline. Without that, the Quaker way to God was closed.

Meeting became a school for faithfulness, a way of directing my attention away from myself towards God, so it would be possible to look for the person God wanted me to be, and into which I had to grow. Simply being there, a part of a loving community with a common experience, gave me great strength. I came to understand why it is impossible to be a Quaker without a meeting. One needs a great basic security to come to God in silence, and the meeting members gave it to me. Moreover, many of them spoke in ministry, and a way of living was offered to me in their words. I had much to learn.

The instrument of my learning was that simple kind of reflection and thought which is called 'meditation'. There is nothing mysterious about it. It is distinguished by its subject matter rather than its technique. I simply thought about God in my life, and at times, increasingly as time passed, my surface reflections and my underlying faithfulness fused together. That is when the Spirit moves and one knows the experience of being searched.

In my own life, it took hard work. I soon learned to spend part of meeting reviewing the week and learning to relax physically. I found what psychology I knew very helpful. I am supposed to be strong and loving, but I know I am often weak and vindictive. Part of the spiritual life is to bring out these things and recognise them, disarming them and offering them to God instead of leaving them in dark, autodestructive secrecy. That is part of being searched—and healed. The same goes for an expression of the anger we all have in us, and hidden antagonism toward members of our own family and meeting. In silence I was able to uncover my illusions.

This process is part of the searching work of the Holy Spirit, the Comforter. Its pain is a necessary part of the mystery, for one is bearing one's own personal cross. Some wise Friends have discerned a sacrificial, and therefore sacramental, significance in worship in stillness. But the Paraclete finishes and fulfills all things. He is the Lord, the Giver of Life.

With time, I began to see the line of my life opening up before me. The space for reflection at meeting helped me to relate my whole being, my soul, to the world in which I am placed, both natural and human. I now go to meeting to face the great questions about how God relates to the creation. I use the language of imagery, myth and the subconscious, scripture and Quaker tradition, family and political life. I go to discover my true self and learn about my part in the great imaginative and creative purposes of God.

Being a particular person, I can only speak for myself. Worship in the unprogrammed Quaker tradition has taught me, I hope, to separate out the important from the trivial in my own life by giving me the space to conduct a dialogue between my own isolation and my need for security. I grew up very slowly, and have usually been too immature for the demands made on me at any particular stage of life. What I have called my conversion happened to me when my religious maturity reached the same stage as my personal maturity. A demand was made on my resources which I had to meet. It was the cross, and my life of worship enabled me to pick it up. It came with the death of my father.

My father was a remarkable man. Like many people from east London, he spent some time at sea and then entered the family trade, in our case, stone masonry. The army turned him from a mediocre artilleryman into an imaginative builder, and he spent the second world war in Egypt learning the skills of management. On several occasions he visited the Holy Land, which made a deep and abiding impression on him. While making a success of business, he retained his socialist convictions, becoming mayor of our town and a highly respected magistrate.

The night he died, I had to take a long look at myself. I had to ask what I really believed. This was the closest death had ever come to me. I had to know whether his measure as a man was solely his contribution to the community, or whether he had gone to an abundant life in the presence of God, where all his manifold and unfulfilled promise would be perfected. I know that the discipline of my worship over the years was inestimably important to me then. I knew how to deal with the grief and all the human consequences, and to set them on one side. When I needed God, I knew how to get in touch instantaneously.

I understood instinctively that my father had been taken into the being of God—to heaven, in a word—and I finally knew that religion was not about me and my problems, but about God. My conversion was almost a literal turning round. I no longer saw heaven as a symbolic representation for our ultimate longings—I came to believe it was a real place. God was there, and so were an awful lot of people, some of whom I had known.

It was all so simple, far simpler than I had ever imagined. I just believed, and that was all there was to be said. But not all there was to be done, for I had to start straightening my life out. I do not remember much sadness in this experience, but a calm joy. I knew that just as my father had lovingly guided me through life, his passing away from it pointed me unmistakably to his, and my, ultimate destination. In the few months following, this realisation made a major difference to my life.

My nature was shown up to me as needing serious alteration. I had been actively involved in politics and had stood for Parliament twice. As a politician, I was sincere about the changes I wanted to see in British society. I still am, but the shift in perspective my father's death brought about showed me that my politics was in large measure protective clothing for an ambition that owed much to the conceit that arose out of my own insecurity. That is not a good foundation for a legislator.

I also learned quite soon that another part of me was a plausible disguise. When people know you have been to Oxford, they expect a certain style, a certain way of applying the brain to the problems of life, whether it be the stock market, crossword puzzles or the practise of religion. Playing up to this had become so habitual that I had failed to see something else my years of quiet meditation had been trying to tell me. I realised with certainty that I was more fundamentally a feeling than a thinking person. I did not have to worry about protecting myself from error by the cultivation of arrogance.

The consequence of all this is that I parted company with my pedestal. I saw through the system that had selected me and schooled me and given me its values and standards. I prized my education highly, but came to reject what it had been for. I discovered the joy of being ordinary. That brought with it a truer sense of people's conditions. No longer was my sense of beauty based on artifice and style, but upon simplicity. Paradoxically it also became clear that the world was in no way as simple as I had thought in my ivory tower. Things were often hard, and sometimes apparently quite meaningless.

These changes were set in train the night I got back from the hospital. I took down the New Testament and read nearly all of it, it seemed, on and on. Actually I must have chosen the familiar parts, but for the first time ever, I heard what it was saying. Instead of using my secular philosophy and attitudes to explain, (or explain away), what was there, I began to take it as the meaning of life and interpret all other things by it. It was coherent, consistent, intelligible. That night I came to know that as Christ was resurrected, so should my father live. For the very first time, I had life in me.

I found that my father's death had caused me unreservedly to commit my life to Christ. Before then I would never ever have used that kind of vocabulary—to do so would have been to lose twenty years of liberal cool. The measure of my conversion is that this no longer matters to me. But if I had not had the search, the finding would not be what it is. When I compare the prodigal son with his elder brother, I reflect that the seed grew best where the soil of hard experience was richest and deepest. Once more, what happened to me was given shape and form by my silent devotions. Over the years I had been growing into the person I now was, by the grace of God.

In a lexicon, the Greek word *metanoia* is used in a variety of senses: a change of thought or feeling; repentance; practical reformation; a reversal of the past; to undergo a change in frame of mind or feeling; to make a change of principle and practise. Each of the above things happened to me. I date my conversion from the act of repentance I made that night. The unreality of death changed my whole attitude towards life.

Since then I have come to realise fully the need to call upon Christ to save me. But one never comes to that experience cold, I believe. In retrospect I see that in the years of still waiting, when God came to me incognito, as it were, God was using my religious exercises to bring me to this point, which I myself would never have foreseen. And when I arrived, I was able to recognise the truth of what was revealed to me, and the rightness of the path by which I had come.

My conversion cannot be explained by the book. Probably no one's can. It was not a movement from no faith to faith, for all the elements of belief were already there. Nor was it a movement from one faith to another, except by stretching the meanings of words. If I had to look for a classical example of my kind of conversion, it is that which happened to Francis of Assisi. He moved from darkness to light, from tradition to reality, from an outward to an inward understanding of what it means to be a

Christian.

Quietly, undramatically, matter of factly, even, I had discovered sin. It was not glamorous or dangerous or thrilling or squalid or extraordinary. It was not being disobedient or breaking the rules or cocking a snook at heaven. It was simply the habit of using your own ego to ignore God, using the numerous resources of your own personality to make yourself the arbiter of your own life, not the One from whom you had it, and to whom it would return. My new-found understanding of my ordinariness meant that I could not disengage myself from the wickedness of the world. I was not superior, I was involved in it. I needed to be saved.

It was a great relief to realise later on that I had come to one of the classical experiences of the Quaker way, but it is a sad censure on Friends in my tradition that nobody had ever told me I might expect it. Part of my conversion was to stop examining scripture for its conformity to the standards of modern enlightenment and to hear what it said about hope, assurance, love and the glory of God. I do not know why supposedly religious people are embarrassed at the thought of being born again. I was, except that Quakerism, the faith of my adoption, traditionally called it 'convincement'.

Quaker convincement was a form of conversion, and originally had nothing to do with being persuaded by experience or force of argument. The word had the same force as our word 'conviction'—the passing of a sentence in a court of law. Friends taught, and had good New Testament evidence for teaching, that Christ was active in all people through what they came to call Christ's inward light. However, the light was not particularly pleasant on first acquaintance, for it illuminated our sins and thereby offered us the possibility of forgiveness and reform.

The imagery of 'light' is full of meaning. If you stand with the westering sun at your back, you see every detail of your shadow thrown on to the road in front of you. That is what you are. That is your shape and dimensions, and you had better get used to it. So with the spiritual light, the activity of the Holy Spirit searching you, the Word of God discerning the thoughts and intents of your heart. Many people turn away, said the early Quakers, preferring what they are to what God is able to make them. But those who respond are saved because they allow themselves to be remade.

Again following the New Testament, early Friends taught the optimistic doctrine that the light, though apparently threatening, was in fact a vehicle of Christ's love and carried with it an assurance of power. If willing to renounce self-centeredness, we would be empowered progressively to abandon all those things which prevent us from entering the fullest communion with God.

Nor were we required to do it all at once. Their genial doctrine of the 'measure', derived perhaps from Romans 12, or Ephesians 4, did not put the same tasks before everybody, nor require the impossible. If you are faithful to that measure of light that you have been given to live up to, they said, more will be given when you are ready. This is a lovely realism.

Though the first Friends held firmly to the view, in theory, that this light could come to anybody without human intermediary, in practise they undertook a far-reaching evangelistic campaign to preach the good news in these terms to the whole world. Testimonies to plainness, opposition to war, and strict honesty expressed in personal conduct were an integral part of this message of salvation and regeneration; they did not offer an experience to others which they had not already undergone themselves. Of the earliest Quaker preachers, William Penn said, "They were changed men themselves before they went about to change others. Their hearts were rent as well as their garments; they knew the power and work of God upon them."

In my case, convincement came after a number of years of membership in the Society. It was set in train by the personal example and testimony of one man. The emotional power of the experience is not in doubt, but I cannot say I displayed the extravagant expression of remorse which once merited the name 'Quaker'. In my case the light went straight to the integral or fundamental me. It brought about a permanent and fundamental change. But its operations were neither instantaneous nor dramatic.

Nowadays, 'convincement' is often used in the intellectual sense of becoming a Quaker, as if convinced or persuaded of the truth of 'Quakerism'. Certainly my own convincement involved my mind. If I had not already understood what was involved in the Christian faith, I would not, I think, have recognised what was happening to me. But convincement is much more than that. It is a sign of continuing revelation of truth; that the God who is the source of this revelation is accessible within; that this God is one who comes seeking our response and our love, but a God who requires the brokenness of will of which Jesus spoke. My conversion was the beginning of real life. I was moved from self-sufficiency to dependence, pride to humility, wilfulness to obedience. I had been searched, and I had discovered the power of silent waiting.

An
Experience
of
Unprogrammed
Worship

An
Hour
to
Fill...

When I first went to Oxford University, I was given rooms high up in a nineteenth-century building that masqueraded as something much more ancient. The older parts of my college went back to the reign of Henry VIII. At that time their plumbing and heating arrangements did too, so I did not complain. In fact there were advantages to being where I was. I was perched up on the skyline in among the dreaming spires, with entrancing views across the city down valleys and canyons of eaves, gables and parapets.

My little set of rooms also gave me a great deal of musical pleasure. Every night as I lay in bed, I heard the chimes ring round the city at twelve o'clock when everything was quiet. Beginning at five to the hour, and not finishing till five past, the bells from the clocks on spire and pinnacle, tower and wall, gave their blessing to the slumbering populace. Like the cadences of the medieval plainchant, they helped my soul to remember its source at the close of the day.

It is strange, then, that this environment should lead my mind away from the outward beauties of faith towards the quiet simplicities of Quaker worship. In Oxford one is close to the heart of the Church of England, its scholarship, architecture and music, its history and its continuity with the common past of Western Christendom. All these things proclaim the greater glory of God and demand in worship and in prayer the best one has to give. Yet, like an independent and seemingly ungrateful child, I chose not to follow the faith of the national church. Instead, one morning I was drawn to the Friends meeting, and I have worshipped among Friends ever since.

I do not know what I expected to find when I went there. I had a hazy notion of what happened in a meeting, and the Quaker students whom I knew all teased me gently when I asked them about it, saying that it was just an uncomfortable hour of sitting still in silence. I suppose I must have had an invitation, because I got there somehow, but it was really out of curiosity that I went. I suppose, in honesty, it was the Testimonies that first attracted me to Quakerism. Very briefly, these say that in all circumstances, no matter how trying, we are under a religious obligation to speak and live truthfully, peaceably and simply.

I have always tried to take the Testimonies seriously and was able to grasp their outlines from the beginning of my life as a Friend. But as time has passed by, my understanding of the setting in which each of them receives its vitality has changed. I have come to appreciate that there is a Quaker understanding of Christian doctrine which deserves to be taken seriously and can carry intellectual weight beyond the Society of Friends. I have also become convinced that within the Society, the silent meeting for worship is the best guarantee that the strength to live up to the Testimonies will continue to be available.

The first thing that struck me about Oxford meeting house was its smell. Churches have to smell, if you think about it, and they all have their own characteristics. You can smell incense in some churches, woodsmoke or the heating system in others. Some smell of the damp. Some smell of dust, particularly if they have an old organ, and lots of curtains and hassocks.

This meeting house had a lot of wooden panelling and benches, so it smelled of furniture polish. I like the smell of furniture polish, so I was disposed to like the meeting. Come to think of it, the benches may have been covered with leather, and I like that too. So I was off to a good start. As I looked around on that first day I ever went to meeting (not realising that 'First Day' was Quaker jargon for what I called Sunday), I saw lots of people who could really only be described as 'plain' in the nicest sense of the word.

What I mean is that those I saw on my way into the room where the meeting took place had a benign expression on their faces and a certain calmness that made me feel relaxed rather than openly welcomed. I suppose 'fellow feeling' is an expression that would describe it. There was no ostentation in their clothes or attitudes. They settled themselves and their fidgety children unselfconsciously into their places without worrying over much (as I would have done) about disturbing those who were already occupied in the odd process of sitting there in quietness. It was not dissimilar to other churches I had known, but I have to remark that in any town there are churches where 'plainness' is not the first word you would think of to describe the worshippers. However, it usually is among Friends, and that applies to both the silent and the worship-service kind.

So here I was, sitting on a bench in a Friends meeting for the first time in my life, not knowing at all what to expect. There was nothing to look at, nothing to occupy my mind, nothing to appeal to my senses, nothing to sing, nothing to join in with, in fact, absolutely nothing whatever to do, and a whole hour to fill.

I imagine that nearly everybody feels like this at their first unprogrammed meeting, for this manner of worship is exceptional. However, one does not have to move for very long in Quaker circles to find that it can speak to the condition of Friends and non-Friends alike. There is a common pattern of experience, whatever the outward religious loyalty of those who come. People will say that at first the silence is highly demanding, but after a while it becomes a source of peace and spiritual nourishment. Those who find they are unable to do without it naturally tend to become Friends. Those who like to come sometimes, but prefer other kinds of worship, are usually friends of Friends. Sitting on my bench, it was not yet clear whether I would fall into either of those groups, for I had no experience of silence whatsoever. So what did I do?

First, I suppose, I did not actually do anything, but something happened. It was not terribly sensational. It was simply the consequence of being well brought up and put in a social situation in which I did not want to make an exhibition of myself. There was no opportunity to stand up and stretch, chat to my neighbour, chuckle, yawn, snore, snort, wriggle, stretch out on the bench, keep turning round to see who was behind me, or do anything that might make a noise and disturb the other people in whatever it was they were doing. I knew they were supposed to be worshipping God, but there was precious little evidence of that happening.

Being deprived of movement, and not a little frightened lest I be responsible for a grunt or a squeak or a sniff that would draw all the eyes in the meeting house upon me, I settled myself as comfortably as I could for a long wait and began to take stock of my surroundings. In the years that followed I was to become completely at home in the atmosphere I experienced that day, but on the first occasion I don't think I did very much worshipping.

I was not used to sitting totally still for a long period of time, so the meeting was quite an experience for me. I remember my astonishment at how I seemed far more aware than usual of all the messages my senses were giving me. It also dawned on me that these messages were there all the time, but I was normally far too busy to pay attention to them.

I was surprised to find the light remarkable, and I do not mean the spiritual variety Quakers like to go on about. After a good few years of membership in the Society of Friends, I have clocked up a pretty fair total of meeting houses attended, and I get the feeling that there is something about the windows that is very important. In meeting houses, they tend to be high up in the eaves, so that shafts of sunlight cascade to the floor, warming the worshipping Friends, colouring the posy of flowers on the central table, or burnishing the gold lettering on the spine of the Bible which also lies there.

Whether or not it was felt in former times that if you had windows to gaze out of, you would lose the art of inward retirement and spend too much time admiring the creation to take notice of the creator, I don't know. When the day is grey or dim, as it usually is in England, and the meeting house has a pitched roof or ceiling, you look up not to obscurity, but to as much clarity as the architecture can scoop out of the day. I do not now remember the state of the weather the day I first went to meeting, but I certainly noticed the light.

Part of the irresistible appeal that churches still have for me is the aura of mystery surrounding what they have in them. The altar, the candlesticks, the coloured glass, the raised pulpit and lectern all speak to me of holiness in the midst of the ordinary. The meeting house was similar. The play of light gave me a sensation of being enclosed or momentarily retired from the outside world rather than being separated from it. The place where I sat was not a refuge in which to wait for the coming of the kingdom, but an outpost of that kingdom in St. Giles' Street, Oxford.

The next thing I was really conscious of was the group of which I was a member. I have already remarked upon the underplayed style of the people among whom I had walked down the garden to the meeting house. I knew that the Quakers had once worn grey clothes without collars and lapels as a sort of uniform. I also knew that they had been such fervent and peaceable people that they courageously accepted prison rather than compromise their beliefs. I did not then appreciate the reasons for these things, but I was aware that their tradition was a living one.

There was little ostentation among them. The silence seemed to emphasize both their uniqueness and their solidarity. There were many variants of the benevolent gaze with which some swept the room. Others maintained an oddly rigid posture for what seemed to me to be an age. Closed eyes completed a frown of concentration on some faces or the blandness of apparent slumber on others. There were the human quirks—the flamboyant blowing of the nose into a gaudy handkerchief, the scratching of the outside of a leg, the unconscious pulling of a face that revealed the presence of a divine blessing or an uncomfortable memory. The odd newcomer like myself clutched an introductory leaflet. In the odd corner people read.

There were none of the usual landmarks of worship. With no organ, piano or order of service, there was no need for a little board hoisted up on high to tell people the numbers of the hymns. Indeed, apart from a Bible and a couple of other volumes peculiar to the Quakers, which were on the table in the middle of the room, there weren't any books at all. Since there was no priest or minister, and one did not expect a public reading of the Bible, it followed that there was no need for a pulpit or a lectern. I rather liked the idea that the benches were arranged in a rectangle round the central table. Sitting at the back, I could see everybody else, and there was nowhere to sit where I would not be directly facing at least a quarter of my fellow worshippers.

I do not think I consciously sat and worked all this out. Rather, it was borne in upon me as I tried to sit still and open myself to the novelty. My reflections were not particularly religious, either. During the hour I prayed a bit and thought a lot about what I took to be divine things, but my mind kept coming back to the simple consciousness of where I was. At that stage of my life it was important simply to be there, and since I had been looking forward to my visit, I expect it was largely childish excitement that made my first meeting memorable.

Much later, I learned that the original meetings in the seventeenth century took far longer than the hour that was scheduled for that morning—indeed the early Friends would have swooned at the very idea of scheduling the length of the meeting. Meeting for worship ended when the Holy Spirit indicated, and not before. But in the time of George Fox and William Penn, there were no trains and buses to catch. People were far more independent and able to dispose of their own time. So on this occasion, the Holy Spirit utilised the wristwatch rather than the inward illumination of the heart to tell the Friends when to break off their devotions.

The manner of starting and finishing were noteworthy too. We drifted into meeting and ended in what was for me a mixture of relief and anticlimax. This was all part of the pattern of having no clergy and no visible organisation. The meeting began when the first worshipper sat down, so the next person to come entered an already living silence. In this way there was no chatter, no theatrical entry to give a clear beginning and no sudden switch of concentration from talking to one's neighbour to talking to God. I don't remember coming late, so I suppose I sat and watched others come in, wondering about them the while.

During my first ever hour in an unprogrammed Quaker meeing, there was what I now know as 'ministry'. After twenty minutes or so, somebody got up and made a short speech. It cannot have lasted more than a couple of minutes, and I came to recognise this as the norm. It was different from the prepared sermon not only in its length but also its style. There were several other pieces of ministry during the hour, and though they were from different voices, the style was the same—short, pithy, illustrated with stories taken from life, and tentative or suggestive in manner rather than definite or authoritative. I never dreamed that I would much later come to admire, imitate and then question this style when I myself was moved to minister in meeting.

So my first meeting was spent largely in looking and absorbing the atmosphere. It was hard work because I was an outsider and I did not want to commit a faux pas. I said a few prayers so I could feel religious and thought hard about what had been said by those who ministered. The bench was even harder than my thoughts, and time began to weigh heavily. At a quarter to the hour I was ready to go, but there was no escape. I had to sweat it out to the end, and I was truly grateful when two people at the front, who I later discovered were elders, ended the meeting by shaking hands. That action was followed by a relieved, but definitely friendly rustle. In the midst of the company, somebody got up and gave the notices and sat down. Hubbub began, and I dodged the Friendly greeters who were bearing down on me and escaped into the street. It had been nothing like I expected, but I went back. It turned out to be one of the big beginnings in my life.

Finding
a
Voice

I went back to Oxford meeting house because the experience I had been through roused my curiosity. Was Quaker worship my path to a deeply spiritual life that was at the same time highly practical? In the bloom of youthful religious enthusiasm, I needed both those things—or at least I needed the assurance that they were available. Here in the meeting, somewhere, was one of their sources, and I felt drawn to try and discover it.

The surroundings were congenial too. I found that the plain architecture and the arrangement of the room used for worship were to my taste. A temperamental nonconformity revealed itself in me. Over the first few weeks of worshipping in silence, I realised that I was no longer able to enter fully into worship that was led by somebody else. This made me sad, and worried me not a little. It was hard to separate this distaste from a suspicion that I was simply being spiritually proud. I learned quickly that silent worship came at a price, and I needed to be sure I had the resources to meet it.

An uncomfortable feeling that was aroused in me was a sense of challenge. Some people attend their first Friends meeting and know straightaway that this is where they belong. They find that the silence refreshes them, and they can somehow sink into its peace. This was not my experience. I found it disturbing and rather troublesome. Used to a structured service, I found myself with no points of reference and nothing to check against. There seemed to be no shape in an unprogrammed meeting, yet I sensed that there was, and that if I persevered, I would find it.

God is infinitely kind and infinitely tactful. As I look back on the religious journey that has taken me deeper and deeper into the stillness of Friends worship, I realise that the quietness does have a shape and a meaning and that God has used it to give my life those things. Over the years I have learned to see and to follow the pillar of cloud and the pillar of fire. I have also learned that the silence has little intrinsic value unless it is put in the setting of the Quaker way of life.

My exploration of Quaker worship became the discovery of this way of living. The practise of the one encouraged the other. I knew nothing of this when I started to go to meeting. As a beginner I naturally sought to use the silence for my own purposes. I had no thought that the silence would come to leave its mark upon me. If my prayers and meditations were stones, it was the silence that formed them into a temple and made them live.

On the surface, a silent meeting appears to be a group of people sitting together but worshipping individually. Some adventurous souls attach themselves to the Society of Friends because they are attracted by the silence. They conclude that Quaker worship is simply an opportunity for meditation. The collective wisdom of the Society has never accepted that view, however, for its evangelical and liberal wings both insist that meeting is a collective activity, as its name ought to indicate. Much of what we do may be personal, but we come before the Lord in a body.

There is really no way to avoid coming to grips personally with the demands made by the silence. This has to be done from the beginning, and it is highly challenging to the dedication and resourcefulness of the worshipper. There is no generally accepted plan, scheme or technique for learning the art of silent worship. The Society of Friends is not like the freemasons. One is not initiated into deeper and deeper mysteries by properly appointed persons when one has shown one's worth and learned the secret lore. I would hazard the generalisation that while one can become highly experienced in Quaker worship, one cannot become *expert* in it.

This lack of direction may be dismaying. One may feel as if one has lost the oars overboard and cannot keep the boat going. In fact, however, the difference of Quakerly opinion about the use of silence is a charter of freedom. One can do what one likes in it without any sense of failure or falsehood, granted an initial sincerity of intention, of course. That is the first and most vital lesson about coming to unprogrammed worship.

It follows from this that learning to worship in the corporate silence of a Friends meeting is not like taking a course of study. There are no tests to see how far one has come or whether one has understood. The most important step forward in the life of prayer is to realise that we are all at the same stage—the beginning— every time we come into God's presence. We can learn many new ways of doing this, and we can adopt the ways that fit our own temperament or inclination. This is the point about experience as against expertise.

We may discover that there is a far wider range of approaches to God than we had imagined. We may well be able to achieve greater depth of devotion as time passes. But we shall never know, when we set out on the adventure of an hour's silence with Friends, or our own quiet time at home, whether that gift of depth will be given to us, or whether we shall once more be beached in the shallows we knew at the very beginning of our pilgrimage of prayer.

To draw sharp distinctions in an attempt to characterise the varieties of Quaker spirituality is therefore a mistake. In the past there have been opposing parties within the Society over the principles of worship. But controversies are seldom clear-cut. I know there are purists who see hymn-singing as a falling away from some pristine ideal of Quaker worship, but I doubt whether it is. There are times when I am suffocated by silence and I yearn for the liberty of scripture and gospel song.

But I also know that there are times when the cosy habits of my religious upbringing prevent me from hearing the voice of God speaking to me because I am drowning it out with the repetition of scripture and the words of hymns that represent experiences I have not yet made my own. What I do know about myself is that I need both. I have simultaneously to be a silent, world-denying Quaker in the traditional mould and an active world-affirming Quaker in the contemporary mould. I do not worry about this because the Christian faith itself has this division at its heart. It is a source of strength, not of weakness.

Back in Oxford, when I first attended meeting regularly, I managed the silence very well by praying and meditating in it. I came with particular things to think about. I was learning about the Quakers and investigating what it would be like to be a Friend. This was done in the silence, but I did not learn until later how the silence itself could alter what I did in it. I came to discover it was this interaction that was characteristic of Quaker spirituality. I invented two terms, beauty and austerity, to describe the ways I thought of my reactions to the world and to the relationships I had with it. They summed up for me the world-affirming and world-denying attitudes that I knew were both part of me. My personal spiritual quest was to keep them in balance.

Beauty and austerity are not the most obvious pair of opposites. The classical mind finds clarity of line and economy of detail the essence of beauty, and, in the artistic sense, I do too. In religion, however, I have experienced beauty as a fulfillment, a richness, a symbol perhaps of spiritual harvest. The colour of an altar at Epiphany, with bright white linen, the silver and gold of the vessels and the winter day outside say things about the richness of divine blessing for which I could never find words. So does the immense majesty in sound of Bach's B Minor Mass.

On the other hand, austerity goes with being stripped down to the essentials, being deprived of everything except what you need to get by—the winter of the soul. I hear austerity in plainchant. I feel it in cold stone and hard benches. I know it because I have been physically impaired for most of my life. It is also a part of the grace of God, but it is a challenge to my selfishness. I need to be saved, but I am afraid of the Cross.

These feelings were only latent in me when I first went to Friends meetings, but over the years they have been watered and nourished so that they now form an important part of my worship. The beauty is easy. Joy comes straight from the heart. The hard part of life, on the other hand, challenges all the common assumptions about who we are and what we need. We can grow from a human to a divine joy, but the way is through austerity. I take these things to be truths, but they are hardly obvious. So I have come to the conclusion that the world of our experience is a subtle place which places great challenges before us.

These two poles of experience illustrate a tension that exists in modern Quaker worship as I have come to understand it. Traditionally, Friends drew a hard and fast distinction between the fallen-ness of our natures, which they called the 'creature', and the inflowing redeeming divine love which they knew as the 'Inward Light'. They taught that we would only be able to hear the voice of God if we cultivated a passiveness towards all the ideas and emotions which crowd into the worshipping mind and learned to listen to God by controlled stilling of our human faculties.

This poses a problem because it is pretty clear that such an understanding of worship is quite different from what goes on in most Quaker meetings today, whether they be of the programmed or the unprogrammed variety. Friends are proud of their heritage and would be very reluctant to deny their spiritual kinship with George Fox, Margaret Fell, William Penn and the others. On the other hand, they would be equally reluctant to be bound by the beliefs and practises of the seventeenth century as if nothing has happened since.

I find the traditional distinction, and the view of human nature on which it was based, unacceptable without considerable qualification, and I am sure most Friends would agree with me. I am a being with a heart, a mind, reason and conscience. I have a memory, resolution, urges and passions and desires. I know when I sin, but I also know when I don't. The idea that all the things that make me the person I am are somehow tainted is unacceptable.

The tradition drew a sharp distinction between inward and outward religion. It saw an opposition between faith engaged with the world and faith engaged with the realm of the spirit. It believed that devotion to hidden realities precluded a concern with the outward expression of the mysteries of belief. It saw silent worship as a sign of these values and the means of protecting them.

I have not resolved this tension in my own life, try as I will. I swing between a preference for one or the other as I see the merits in each. I find myself in dialogue with my own tradition. While I have to make a basic commitment to the Quaker understanding of the religious life, I also find myself developing a critical commentary on it. It is sometimes comforting to reflect that the tension is present across the Quaker divide in both the programmed and unprogrammed communities.

With the unprogrammed tradition, for example, many Friends find a solid basis for their religious lives in the philosophy and practise of some form of social action. Much of their worship seems to comprise meditation on the implications of the effort to make the world a better place and how they can play their part with others in such a great endeavour.

This attitude has a sound biblical basis (though many of its practitioners are indifferent to the fact), and has roots in the Quaker tradition. But it is not the whole of it. Friends of former times were gravely suspicious of making common cause with other people in case it led to a weakening of the Quaker peculiarities, notably the importance of waiting on God for individual guidance rather than using reason or our native wit. Social activist Quakerism is of great value, but spiritually it is essentially 'outward'.

So is much of the programmed tradition. Some time ago, I attended an Easter service at a Friends church in Indiana. Many of those who were there had been up for an Easter dawn vigil and then come along to the meeting at which there was what can only be described as heavenly choral music. The theme of the meeting was the triumphant release brought us by Christ. During the open worship—the silence at the heart of a well-constructed programmed meeting—there was a piece of ministry from a member of the congregation which took the form of a testimony to God's grace at work in his family. He began, "As the grandson of a slave..." I cannot begin to describe how moving this was for English ears. The whole service made its impact, quite properly I believe, by its appeal to the emotions through imagery and music. Just like the previous kind of Quakerism, it was engaged with the world, and would have been equally offensive to the tradition.

Ironically, if we can find Friends in both the programmed and the unprogrammed traditions whose practises emphasize our engagement with the world as well as with God, there are also Friends within each group who are close to the tradition of non-engagement. One of the strangest features of contemporary Quakerism is the number of Friends who are surprised to discover how much they have in common with Catholics and high Episcopalians.

This link certainly existed in years gone by, when the seventeenth century quietist writers were widely known among Friends. Nowadays, a common interest in mystical religion and an appreciation of the insights on Jungian psychology reinforce this community of interest. There is a strong sense in these quarters of the inwardness of religious experience, the importance of symbolism and the integration of the personality as a path to God.

Though stemming from quite different roots, it is possible to argue that the holiness movement, so important in certain Quaker circles, is a programmed tradition counterpart of these trends. Certainly it has a theology far removed from what is generally considered to be the Quaker position, but it cannot be denied that emphasis on the second work of grace is an intensely personal matter and a gift only vouchsafed after a considerable period of personal discipline and inward striving. You can not really ask for a more inward expression of religion than this.

The implications of these things are upsetting for the conventional wisdom among Friends. This holds that the programmed tradition, inheriting the legacy of the nineteenth century frontier revivals, practises an 'outward' form of worship, where Friends of the unprogrammed tradition worship in silence and are therefore 'inward'. Such an analysis permits heated argument as to which branch is the true guardian of the Ark of the Quaker Covenant.

On the other hand, it could be that the Religious Society of Friends cannot be divided down the middle on organisational or theological grounds in this way. Perhaps there are many more Friends like me than I realise, caught in a creative tension between a tradition they want to belong to and the need to apply it to the challenges of modern life. If that is so, the argument about programmed and unprogrammed worship is divisive, antiquated and beside the point. There are more important things for Friends to be getting on with. When I first went to Quaker meetings for worship, I was looking for a voice in which I could speak comfortably to God. Now I have found it, I hear its echoes in all branches of the Society of Friends.

Speaking
Comfortably
to
God

My first steps in the silence were taken in prayer. That was something I already knew how to do. The simple acts of self-examination, confession, thanksgiving, praise, intercession and petition allowed me to give some sort of shape to what I was doing, and thereby increased my confidence. Moreover, they were part of a heritage. Since my earliest years I have lived among people to whom they were important. The desire to possess them for myself, to find their power, was the first task I put my hand to in the silent meeting.

I was undertaking an apprenticeship rather than a process of learning. It matters to me to put it that way, because I am trying to describe something I did rather than something I thought about. It was not always easy, but it was rewarding. Faced with an hour of silence, I did the only thing I could. I called on the resources of prayer I already had and began to work at them. However crowded the week was—and I was very bad at routine and the regular quiet time—I knew that with Sunday would come a gruelling and exciting exposure to the searching wind of the Spirit. After nearly thirty years of these weekly periods of quiet, I can see beneath the surface of my youthful intentions. The meeting house became my cloister.

God is love, as St. John reminds us. This short phrase must be absorbed into the soul of anyone wishing to follow the Christian

way. Like so many—one is tempted to say, all—the truths of the
faith, it is capable of being received superficially, or after great
struggle. The one is the form of religion, the other the substance
of it. One of the difficulties with which most of us strive is that we
find it hard to love ourselves. Yet why should we? Our faith
promises us that there are no limits to God's love for us, so how
can there be any limits to our own lovableness?

I have learned more about God by being a parent than anything
else in my experience. Humanly speaking, I know that self-respect
and self-esteem are the greatest gifts I should try to give my son
and my daughter. In my prayer life, my intimacy with God, I
stand as a child, though a grown one. How much more, then,
should I strive to find that lovableness in my soul which God
created for himself?

So much in our cultural heritage and our psychological
development is harmful to our confidence and our image of
ourselves that we must begin our worship with an increasing self-
knowledge and self-love. It is as if some Old Testament voice says,
"Who is this that stands before me?" We should be able to answer
with confidence, so self-examination must be our constant
concern.

Perhaps my picture of self-examination owes more to twentieth-
century psychology than traditional spirituality. In terms of
technique and purpose, it may. But in its most important respect,
it does not. The soul is to be understood as that which responds to
God. It is wider than the mind. It includes what we are to become,
as well as what we are.

This distinction is important, for prayer is growth toward God.
One of the obstacles to self-love is that our ideas about
wrongdoing have gone off the rails somewhere. St. John also
wisely reminds us that if we say we have no sin we deceive
ourselves and the truth is not in us. There are many layers of
meaning in this saying. Certainly it asserts the sinfulness of
human nature. But why not? G.K. Chesterton said that original
sin is the only Christian doctrine open to empirical verification,
and he had a point. After all the argument, hurting other people
and feeling guilty about it is something we all do—and need to be
freed from.

However, it is guilt that is the big problem, not sin. The
conscience could not operate without it, so it does have its uses.
Nevertheless, if it teaches us we are miserable and depraved, it

has been allowed to go way beyond its proper function. It will then prevent us from knowing that we are lovable and put paid to any chance of growing into the people God wants us to be—the discovery, as some people put it, of our true selves. So we need to deal with our guilt, to be able to keep growing, and to be reconciled constantly both with God and our neighbour.

One of the discoveries I made through self-examination and confession is that the Christian faith is for failures. I do not mean that we are absolved from striving for the highest moral and spiritual standards, but that properly understood, this faith will protect us from self-doubt, self-reproach and guilt when we fail to achieve what we think we should. Faith is not about the acceptance of dogmatic truth, it is about rising above our limitations. That is the sense in which we can be saved and why any doctrine of justification by works is a return to legalism and bondage.

At meeting, I began to explore the nature of this kind of faith. It appeared to be a combination of things like hope, trust, love, and the simple confidence that in the long run, somehow, everything will be all right. I was learning that faith had to do with the response of the heart, and with the confession that I am not as God would have me be. And that was a relief, for I learned that if we are honest, we are taken into God's confidence. So now, as in my early days, meeting for worship necessarily involves a long look at myself, and the confession that is good for the soul. I emphasize confession, because it helps me to get guilt out of the way and to deepen my relationship with God.

Another thing that takes a great deal of time is thanksgiving. This is not very sharply distinguished from praise in my own mind, and I have heard it described as the only possible response to the overflowing love of God. As with confession, I have to be careful not to use these words in a juvenile sort of way. Thanksgiving is not the obsequious self-abasement of an insecure courtier. Praise is not shabby flattery designed to ingratiate. Both these activities of prayer are far removed from that. They relate to intimate love, not formal relationship.

So I came to realise that the best way to deepen my love of God was to use my experiences of the love in my everyday life in all its variety, subtlety and uncertainty. Getting on with those I love is often a business demanding patience, discretion, tact and under-standing. It gets complicated sometimes. It also gets strained, occasionally to the breaking point. But without expression, it is barren. I show my love in the things I do, and I also show it by words of endearment. These things are all part and parcel of one another. This is what worship should be like. This is the idiom in which we should speak to God.

Of the other two traditional kinds of prayer, intercession for the needs of others and petition for one's own needs, there is nothing to be said in short. I cannot debate the question whether prayer 'works'. I can only say that, regardless of the result, I do pray for other people. What I have learned through years of stillness is part of the austerity of faith. If I take Christ's teaching about humility seriously, whenever I am moved to ask something for myself, I find that I am first praying for others. This matters to me. It took many years to learn. What opened the gates of asking God's blessing on others and help for myself was the dawning of my awareness that when Jesus told us to ask, he meant it. Moreover, if we are to pray for others, we ought also to pray for ourselves and not be silly about it.

In those first meetings before I left the university, I was quite self-centered and used the silence for prayer. I still do, for prayer is the foundation of faith. For much of the time in meetings, I am going through these religious exercises. They nourish me, and I hope, enable me to grow. They are not the whole story, though. The Quakers talk a lot about silence and worship, but the tradition of silent prayer goes much further back into the history of the church than the comparatively recent emergence of the Religious Society of Friends.

There is a quality about the silent meeting which goes beyond personal devotions. Our relationship with God stretches two ways. We come into the sanctuary alone, needing to make our peace, but the conditions on which we do so derive from something wider than our own personal needs. We are not islands of consciousness, fragments of understanding, solo voices of praise, pieces of moral rectitude. Within the sanctuary we join with others. We become a people. We hear together. We minister to each other's needs on behalf of the One we have come to worship.

This aspect of Quaker worship is learned with time. It can be argued that the survival of the Society of Friends depends on historical chance alone. If that were so, its characteristic form of worship would be rewarding for those who practise it, but scarcely distinctive. I was not aware of these deeper things when I was a student at the beginning of my spiritual search. But as time passed I began to realise that there was more to silent worship than undisturbed prayer. It was not simply a medium for my religious self-expression. It imposed a discipline. To sustain the discipline, a way of life was necessary. For the way of life to carry conviction and power, a faith was necessary. Quakerism, I came to see, was expressed most eloquently in the silence. But to see the silence as the defining characteristic was to put the cart before the horse.

One way of summarising this story is to say that I was gaining experience of the silent meeting. 'Experience' is a word Friends are fond of using when discussing their faith with others, and it needs to be thought about a little. It often occurs in Quaker writings, and since it is capable of a number of meanings, it is sometimes misinterpreted. What exactly do we mean by 'spiritual experience'?

For many people, the most immediate and obvious meaning of the word is to describe feelings, our subjective emotional responses to the things that go on around us and provide the colour in our lives. This is obviously a fundamental. Whatever else I will admit to, I know that I am a stream of consciousness perpetually responding to a stream of stimuli. In all sorts of ways my feelings involve me in the world beyond myself. I 'experience' it.

But there is a wider sense of the word also. If we are not content just to receive whatever the world sends us, we must reflect on the significance of the events we are a part of and move our understanding of 'experience' beyond the merely subjective. If we have thought about ourselves at all, we will have come to the point at which we have to reach some fundamental decisions about what we take the world to be like and what we conceive our place in it to be. Such reflections are also entitled to be called 'experience'.

These fundamental convictions are important. Since we base our lives on them, they are rather more than guesses, opinions, conjectures, or hunches. There is a world of difference between a philosophy of life and a shot in the dark. Often a great deal of anguish and trial has gone into the making of them, and hard knocks too. The reflections that help us to build up our experience must be based on knowledge and thinking that is neither incoherent nor unreasonable. Even more important, they must be sufficiently strong to withstand convention and the pressures to conform that are often brought to bear on us.

Nor is that all. There is more to thinking than simply carrying out the operations we can build a computer to do. Reason is more than being rational. It involves the endeavour to live as a whole being, not just a brain that drives a skeleton. We all of us know that there are chances in life, imponderables, luck, perhaps, the way things are that we cannot put into words. This recognition does not deny the necessity of reasoning, but what it does assert is that there are also other ways of sensing how the world is. Intuition and insight are precious gifts, more usually associated with wisdom than an analytical mind.

Our experience of the world involves knowledge and reason, intuition and insight, and if we want to be balanced, we must give attention to all four. The religious life requires this, of course, for it can only be lived by those who develop their capacity to respond and change.

This was the formative process which the Quaker meeting was subjecting me to in those years that I spent in silent struggle. The spiritual experience that came to me was not so much the beautifully gathered or awkwardly challenging meetings to which my emotions responded, but the slow, continuous formation of my consciousness by the practice of prayer and the discipline of waiting on God.

So I see experience as a flow of understanding, not sliced up responses to particular events. I would guess that it has at least three features. The first is that we are in continuous adjustment to the demands the world makes on us, and the concessions it makes to us, because fundamentally we are also a part of it. The second is that we have a basic choice—we can grant or withhold conscious commitment to it—for it lays obligations on us which we are in a position to accept or decline. Third, we have to be willing to change our understanding and our response to our discoveries and its revelations. We must constantly open ourselves to growth and change.

Anyone with an ear for what is being said can read these things on almost every page of the New Testament. From the time of his first appearance in public ministry, Jesus calls on people to change. When he talks about the kingdom of God, over and over again he uses images of growth. He scorns those who know the weather signs but cannot read the meaning of the political and religious life of their own day. Paul, likewise, in his most majestic passages talks of a new world coming to birth, or of our becoming, in Christ, a new creation. So any worship that reinforces the status quo, either in ourselves or in the Church, is open to the criticism that it is untrue to life—it is not based on experience.

What I have said about experience so far is based on another judgment about what I am and thus how I worship. Certainly I am at times an intellectual, reasoning person. This is an important mode of being. I am an emotional and physical person too. But these sides of my nature are separated out for convenience, nothing more. The essential 'I' is in all these. I know myself to be an integrated whole that is more than the sum of the parts. There is something in me that is comprehensive and total. It takes my questions of my own identity, my place in the cosmos, and my moral obligations and seeks a balance that satisfies me and makes sense to me. The old fashioned among us call it 'the soul'. That is what we worship with. It is what we use to speak comfortably to God.

A
Witness
to the
Truth

Openness to growth and change is the key to a life of experience rather than habit or insularity. That is easily said, but the process of opening up can be a tricky one. Natural prudence suggests to many people that sudden changes are likely to be risky and that solid change is gradual. Moreover, when things happen at a leisurely pace, it is sometimes difficult to register the distance one has come.

The formative influence of the meeting operates within these constraints. It is misleading, therefore, to give an account of Quaker worship which overemphasizes what happens to the individual's flow of consciousness during one single span of sitting in silence. That experience by itself is receptive rather than transforming. What matters is what one learns to do in the stillness over an extended period.

In the silence of a gathered meeting, religious seekers have always found a discipline which disarms the sentimental feelings and habits of mind which arise from self-centeredness. This really is the key to the early Quaker experience. Robert Barclay wrote in 1676, "For, when I came into the silent assemblies of God's people, I felt a secret power among them, which touched my heart; and as I gave way unto it I found the evil weakening in me and the good raised up; and so I became thus knit and united unto them, hungering more and more after the increase of this power and life whereby I might feel myself perfectly redeemed; and indeed, this is the surest way to become a Christian..."

In the long term it has always been Friends' experience that we must accept the discipline of will which seeks to overcome our natural self-centeredness. Our emotions and sentiments always have to run to keep up with what we know to be true, and that is sometimes painful. But it is the essence of the thing. Robert Barclay's encounter with silence showed him where the power to change was to be found and brought about his personal transformation.

In contemporary terms, I suppose we could describe it as adopting a discipline of detachment: severing the bonds from whatever the unreflective part of ourselves tries to bend to its use to prevent the soul from opening itself to God. This, of itself, carries a power, for it is an irrevocable decision, a leap of faith, a way of liberation. It opens us to the possibility of redemption from our own emotional and physical limitations and the narrowness of our moral vision. For me, like Barclay, this is an experience of the real presence of Christ in the meeting, perpetually calling me to choose Christ's way and not the world's.

So in the stillness of meeting, every time and all the time, we are being called to centre our lives in God's will, not our own. This is partly to do with how we resolve our own natural moral dilemmas, partly how we utilise properly the legitimate freedom which God has given us, and partly how we accept the human obligations life sends our way. By our own meditations, and also by abandoning ourselves to the divine presence, we meet the challenges and receive the power. It may not be dramatic, but it is real.

The development of the Quaker Testimonies is possibly the clearest example of how the process of spiritual formation through silent waiting actually works. The Testimonies express the public, or political, aspects of Quaker faith. They make a diagnosis of the human condition which asserts an indissoluble link between what happens in the individual and what happens in social systems composed of individuals. The Testimonies do not accept that the evils in the world can ultimately be traced back to 'the system' and say that when individuals wish to change, society can—and not before. The primary appeal of the social reformer must therefore be to the individual conscience.

Ever since I first came among Friends, I was attracted to the Testimonies as an ideal. I wanted to belong to a church which made the rejection of warfare a collective commitment and not just a personal option. I admired a simplicity, a devotion to equality, and a respect for others which reflected what I already knew of Christ. In a deceitful world I warmed to those who did not swear oaths and strove to tell the truth in all circumstances. But this was a beginning in the spiritual life. The seed that was sown in my mind and my politics germinated and struck root in my soul and my faith.

The choice of the word 'Testimony' is instructive. The Testimonies are ways of behaving but are not ethical rules. They are matters of practise but imply doctrines. They refer to human society but are about God. Though often talked about, they lack an authoritative formulation. Though they are not a matter of words, it is through them that the unprogrammed branch of Quakerism does most of its preaching and that the distinctive Quakerism of the programmed tradition is demonstrated.

A 'testimony' is a declaration of truth or fact. Specifically, it is the story a witness tells in court, for the word comes from the Latin word for 'witness'. It is also a particular form of speaking in the churches of the Reformation in which people get up and tell (bear testimony) to what God has done in their lives. Thus, it is not an ejaculation, a way of letting off steam or baring one's soul. It has a purpose, and that is to get other people to change, to turn to God. Such an enterprise, be it in words or by conduct and example, is in essence prophetic and evangelical.

So it is a serious business to adopt the Testimonies. The seriousness comes not through any outward act or sign of adoption visible to other people, but in the implications. On the definition I have suggested, the Testimonies are not just moral challenges or statements about what people may find wise, expedient, agreeable or politically desirable in this world. They carry with them an implication that they are definitive, because they express what God wants. I did not make these things my own until they had been fired in an experience of the world made intelligible by deep reflection and leading in the meeting for worship.

When God decided to make me a lawyer, I misread his intentions entirely. I was at a time in my life when I was dissatisfied with the job I was doing. I had a pretty fair prospect of election to Parliament, and I knew an attorney through my political contacts who would take me on as a clerk and pay me at the same time. It looked a good bet, so I took it, thinking that thereby I would gain some security in the uncertainties of politics, and a reasonable sort of income.

When I entered on my clerkship, I wanted to use the law as a means to achieve social justice. I spent my time getting damages for people who had been injured at work and defending people who were charged with crimes (usually theft) which arose out of their work and of which they were not infrequently innocent. I was encouraged to come across other Quaker lawyers and found that a Friend had written one of our standard English legal texts.

I learned much during this period, but changes were going on inside me. After a few years I gave it all up and moved on. As I now look back, I realise I was going through a process in which God was using the challenges of the job to teach me the meaning of the Quaker Testimonies from life rather than through the influence of the Society of Friends. That meant that what I learned was earthed in reality and was not the attitudinizing of a cloistered virtue that had never been in any moral danger.

The challenge involved power. In both my civil and criminal cases, I saw how the power of the state and the power of wealth can make a thousand trivial injustices add up to one big injustice. My job was to use what power the law gave me to hit back by using the same means of manipulation and coercion that were available to my opponents. I approved of what I did, but, as time went by, it became difficult. I had to face the fact that settling differences by power rather than persuasion is called violence, and I was serving a system that I ultimately rejected. Though my work was not war, it was not peace.

The second challenge involved compromise. Much of my time was spent in negotiating the settlement of claims for compensation, and I usually did this on the basis of what my opponent took the strength of my case to be, not what it actually was. So some clients got more than they ought in justice to have had, others got less. The name of the game was what you could get away with. The procedure was not dishonest, but neither was it the truth, and I became increasingly unhappy with my part in it.

The third challenge involved words. I learned caution and precision. I learned to create verbal thickets and fogs of ambiguity in which to lose both clients and opponents. What lay behind this was the need to protect myself, my firm and my clients, at all costs. Simplicity meant vulnerability, openness, voluntarily closing down options and escape routes. Simplicity meant probably having to carry the can. I was not allowed to be simple.

I thought, and still think, that the quest for justice is something noble, and worth the struggle. The great lawmakers of history made what I was doing part of a grand design that went beyond my own small matters. But when I went home in the evening, it was my own small matters that became something I could not live with. The fact that I could justify the system at large did not mean I could justify my own part in it to myself. So I had to go. In the period during which I made up my mind to leave, I spent much of the time mulling over these things in meeting for worship. That was the hard way God taught me the nature of the Testimonies.

Changing careers for the second time in one's life is a sign of something—instability, to say the least. When I decided that the change had to be made, the time of meeting was a strange blessing, unhurried but stony. I listened within to try to hear the divine voice. I had to be pretty sure my own moral scruples did not do serious harm to my wife and children. I had to come to terms with my fears. I had to allow the point of decision to approach and to meet it with confidence, having weighed up the consequences for all concerned. I had to learn to put my future in the hands of God.

Again, I need to stress that silent contemplation by itself would have done nothing for me. My struggle was not to make sense of my own interior life—I was striving to discern the will of God, and without belief and faith I would have come to grief, I am sure. The belief I relied on was the central doctrine of Quakerism—that the light of Christ is a sure guide to life, and that in the gathered meeting, Christ is present to teach his people (including me) himself. In the stillness of meeting, I heard the voice of the shepherd because I had the sheep's ear.

My striving for clarity as to what I should do, with my heart and soul directed to God, was primarily conducted in meeting, in the place where all the values I had voluntarily chosen could challenge those lesser values which I brought with me. Out of this conflict I found a way forward. It was not through reasoning. During the whole period, coming from meeting, I knew that strength was being given, that I was being supported, that my discernment was true, that my courage was not bravado.

This was an intimation of the Way of the Cross, a spiritual purgation that tested me to see whether my religious commitment was only on the surface. I think that this is a neglected aspect of worship in unprogrammed Friends meetings, but I am sure it was an important part of the tradition. Jesus said that those who are willing to lose their lives will find them. It is easy to say that one is so willing, but another thing to prove it. There is no way out of the occasional, but necessary agony of silent worship unless it be the power of resurrection. When I had been through this period I was another sort of person, and I think I now know why the Testimonies are ultimately inconceivable without the formative experience of traditional Quaker worship.

The reason lies in the process whereby a spiritual experience becomes a political obligation. The Testimonies are essentially prophetic and evangelical. What happened to me was that through the values which I had absorbed half-consciously through Quaker life and the meeting for worship, that prophetic and evangelical challenge was brought to bear when the circumstances arose in which I needed to hear it. Taking the long view I can see that it came at a turning point. If I had not changed the pattern of my life then, I am sure I should have had much misery in later years.

I heard the challenge in my conscience, which is the lodestone of honest living. The conscience as a guide to life is disturbing, troublesome and painful. I guess most of us find it too painful, so to a greater or lesser extent we try to create a personality that is at variance with the one we have been given. This creates discomfort when our experience throws out hints or suggestions that what we are doing is not being honest with ourselves. We do things out of character, and the pull of conscience tells us that this is not how things ought to be.

The barrier we erect to defend ourselves from conscience is a sense of our own self-importance, or pride—the worst of the seven deadly sins. Pride is a form of personal untruthfulness, a way of avoiding the need to recognise the person we really are, and what we stand in need of. It is a device for dealing with fear, but usually only increases it.

Pride comes into play when we feel threatened by the need to change. It is a refusal to see ourselves with God's eyes, a defence against the fear of knowing ourselves. It is the most intractable fear of all. If the meeting for worship is going to have any formative effect whatever, it has to deal with such things in the people who come to it. Friends cannot realistically claim that their faith is built on personal experience if that experience is so refined or recondite that it does not partake of what everybody else knows is the human condition.

Not in abstract, but in the particular circumstances of my life, I had to face these matters. I had to place myself under God's scrutiny, and like Job, return an answer. To others, as well as to me, the Testimonies raise ultimate questions about the nature of individual and social life. They are often revolutionary in their effects, as the gospel is revolutionary by its nature, so I, and those like me who seek to change the world in faithfulness to the Testimonies need to be prepared for the reception given to the one who tried before us.

The Testimonies have to be judged by the extreme case. To witness for peace by accepting prison for refusal to pay taxes for armaments carries a heavy cost. Optimism or a faith in the political process is unlikely to sustain such witness in the long run. Something more is necessary. In meeting and out of it over those months, I was being asked whether I had that something more. The only possible answer was that of Job. When I realised that this was so, I could not quite say with a full heart, "I know that my Redeemer liveth," but I desired to.

And so it is with the ultimate witness. The hostility that always meets Friends' struggle for social betterment arises from exactly the same source as that which Friends have within themselves. Friends have always been able to forgive, because they know that their Testimonies bring a challenge to the pride of the world, and it is only natural that those to whom they speak should discern a threat to their own inward integrity. That is understandable, and forgivable, because on the stony pathway of silent worship, Friends have had the same experience. But where they have been able to crucify their own pride, they have released springs of that divine love with which God redeems the world.

The
Leaven
and the
Heavenly
Light

The kingdom of heaven is a world turned upside down. Hard though it is to our ears, thieves and prostitutes enter it before the conventionally righteous. Labourers who work for five minutes get the same wages as their fellows who have sweated all day. Children are wiser than their elders, beggars are honoured guests at the feasts of kings. The blind see, the dumb speak, the dead are restored to the world of the living.

This catalogue of wonders reads like one of those pictures in which hundreds of things are happening all at the same time in different parts of the same scene. Such things may exist in an imaginative world somewhere, a realm of fancy, but they can scarcely be understood as a description of the solid reality of the here and now.

Yet these are the terms in which Jesus speaks to us. In images, metaphors, snatches of proverb and poetry, wisecracks, aphorisms, tall tales, allegories and thumbnail sketches, he portrays a realm where the only king is God, the only law is love, and the only visa for entry a humble and a contrite heart. He tells us that we carry a passport to the kingdom in our hearts. All we have to do is take it out and use it.

Christianity is not nowadays expressed in terms like this because we tend to be happier with cut and dried statements about religion that look as if they can be proved. This is because so many people really want religion to be science and are apprehensive that they will not be able to find their feet in an upside down world. They cannot put two incongruous things together. Oil and water don't mix, they say.

But they do. All you need is to know how to emulsify them. When you make what in England is known as 'French' dressing, you put the oil and vinegar in the bowl and then add a pinch of mustard. You stir well, and it does the trick. You can season the mixture with pepper and salt, but that just makes it more interesting. You taste oil, you taste vinegar. They are separate but they are the same.

That is how it is with rainbows, or holograms on credit cards, or shot silk which shows different colours according to where you see it from. So it is with the kingdom of heaven. Once you are in it, you can move back and forth again into the 'real' world almost at will, because you know that these are not two different universes but two aspects of the same thing.

To sit in silence and try to worship is inevitably to have an experience like this, to feel the tidal flow of attention and inattention, remembrance and forgetfulness, a sense of the secular and the holy cheek by jowl, a faith that might move mountains, and the wry thought that religion is a hoax and one's devotions a self-indulgent sham. That is the way of it. If one tries to suppress the frivolity, scepticism, boredom or whatever else, one loses the puzzlement that is inseparable from the kingdom.

The influence of this experience is hard to chart, because it has to do with moods and attitudes rather than thoughts. It is a strength of this way of worship that one is not confined to what can be expressed in words, or even in music. The fourteenth-century English hermit, Richard Rolle writes:

> For that sweet spiritual song is very special, and given only to the most special! It is not an affair of those outward cadences which are used in church and elsewhere; nor does it blend much with those audible sounds made by the human voice and heard by physical ears; but among angel melodies it has its own acceptable harmony, and those who have known it speak of it with wonder and approval. (*The Fire of Love*, Penguin 1972, p. 147)

My experience of unprogrammed meeting in the manner of Friends has been important to me by encouraging an exploration of this strange world of complementary opposites, and how to live in it. I am well aware of the opposites in myself, and they often cause a spiritual tension. I experience conflicts between what I am and what I would like to be. I have trouble in distinguishing the significant from the trivial. I feel guilty and irresponsible by turns. In this world such contradictions are intolerable. But if I slip into the kingdom when I cannot make sense of the here and now, I find wheat growing together with tares, and I know that there I am valued for myself, and my failures don't matter.

The stillness has encouraged me to look at the world of my experience like this. I have learned to reflect on the great themes of life and to complete them with the gospel. I have therefore learned much about the person I really am, and have shed, snake-like, the personality I once made for myself. This was a gift of God to me, not an achievement, so I have no worries about it, and I can now live in God's power and not my own. I am not afraid to be angry and bitter; the salvation brought me by the Christ of the silence is that these feelings are recognised, acknowledged, set aside, and disarmed.

So worship without words has as potent a power to shape the individual, to give expression to the deepest feelings, as any other kind. It also has an advantage which is necessarily surrendered when Christians offer worship in the words and formulations of their faith. It is a basis on which those of different faiths can come before God with integrity. One of the greatest paradoxes of the kingdom is that all true faiths are one.

The city of Birmingham, England, where I live, is one of the most racially and religiously mixed communities in Europe. It has a stimulating, challenging and exciting atmosphere. On one occasion, at a big interfaith gathering, I was being very Quakerly and very enlightened. The discussion was about prayer, and I confessed that it was my habit to pray anywhere and that I could do so sitting comfortably in a chair. A devout Muslim woman in the conference was shocked at what she saw as my easygoing familiarity with God, my lack of respect, my denial of my own human dignity. When you think of God, she said, there is only one possible response. It is to go down on your *knees*.

I recognised the truth in what she said and have acted on it ever since, though I regret I have not yet been brave enough to kneel in the meeting house. That will come. From this unnamed woman I learned something of Islam—submission to God—in a way that no Christian had ever taught me. But the words are immaterial. It was not the Mosque or the Koran addressing me, but the living God I know in Christ speaking through her.

I have come to know this living God by immediate revelation, not by inspecting the evidence left behind in written records or by finding what clues there might be to God's character in nature. I am sure that reason and observation, ministry, preaching and scripture can point me towards God, but I have not found them a substitute for direct experience. I realised the true extent of my faith when I became convinced and belief involved my whole soul, not just my mind or heart. I was convinced of, and by, what Quakerism calls 'Truth'. The harmony of my experience and what I have been taught shows me the truth is Christ, so wherever I encounter truth, under whatever guise, there I find Christ waiting for me. The Muslim woman spoke the truth and was thus a minister of Christ.

We can define religion as statements about Truth, for we surely need to be able to talk about it. But irritatingly, we cannot then 'prove' or 'evaluate' one of these statements against another, for none of them contains the standard by which they are to be judged. Practises, scriptures, hierarchies, music, literature, doctrines and symbols all relate to the truth. They can lead us to it, but they leave us at the threshold of understanding. Beyond lies the mystery. Only faith can lead us in.

Truth is the greatness in all things and is beyond my powers of description and analysis. If I think about truth in the narrow sense, I know that things can be true. But I also know that every time I learn something new, I also get a different perspective on what is already there in my memory and understanding. There is always more. So the search for truth is a constant revelation of God's being. Our understanding constantly approaches it, but must not be mistaken for the real thing.

Moreover, we need discrimination. The truth varies in its importance or significance. There are times when it is challenging or intolerable. Moreover, it does not come to us all at once. God prepares us to understand what he wants to impart to us. We are matured to receive God's word, given courage to receive God's challenge, strength to meet God's demands. But we are always left alone to decide whether to respond. That is our free will.

The moral of this is highly important. It is God who saves, not religions, even our own, which is ultimately a human instrument. Quakerism is historically very touchy on this point, for waiting on God in stillness is a reminder that there is such a constant tendency for human instruments and institutions to fall into error and lose their vitality. There is a need for constant watchfulness. Unprogrammed worship builds this possibility into the structure of Quaker church life. It is part of being a Friend of Truth, for the name the Quakers early took for themselves was, 'Friends of Truth'.

It is easy to see how Christianity can deny that other faiths can offer a means of salvation and a way to God. Such a denial is questionable, however, on impeccably orthodox grounds. Early Quakerism had a very high view of the uniqueness, the person and nature of Christ. But it was not afraid to assert that salvation did not depend on an outward knowledge of his life and teaching. It used scripture to present Christ as a fulfillment, not a negation.

I am content to make it my point of departure, for I have to start from the reality of the multi-racial city in which I live, with its diversity of faiths. How can I live as a Christian in a multi-religious world? If there is no other name given under heaven by which we are to be saved, how can the Hindus and Sikhs and Muslims be acceptable to God when they appear to deny that which I have come to believe is the fundamental expression of the divine nature?

I have a problem because my personal faith is Christian, not whatever there is in Christianity that does not conflict with anybody else's faith. I do not care to select those things I find congenial and discount the rest. So I face the implications of the great commission as a commandment given to the Church. To say that people's religion depends on where they live, and I am Christian because I am British, is to look through the wrong end of a telescope. My Northumbrian ancestors needed an Aidan to come from Ireland and convert them from a barbaric polytheism. For me to deny the claims of Christ would be to renounce the faith, to deny its raison d'être.

I could avoid this problem by downgrading my own convictions. I could say, "I may be mistaken, but..." and mean it. That is the sort of religiosity no faith could tolerate. We will not be willing to die for a matter about which we may be mistaken. Alternatively, I could take the option of explaining religious differences as confusions over words and blame language as the source of differences, so that if we could find an appropriate terminology we might all agree.

On the other hand, I could go along with those Christians for whom there is no problem. Such people believe that those who do not confess Christ with their lips are lost. Many such, including Quakers, have left enduring memorials to their love in the schools and hospitals their missions have supported. This move would preserve my faith in Christ intact, but would the Christ of my devotion be the figure revealed in the gospel?

I think not. Jesus declared that there are many mansions in heaven. To assert that we can be entertained there by those who found God in the gurdwara, the mosque or the temple is a legitimate interpretation of the life and teaching of Christ, and I make it. Through Isaiah, God says, "...this people draw near me with their mouth and honour me with their lips, while their hearts are far from me." This is the death-knell of literalism.

The Quaker tradition seems to me to resolve this character-istically modern problem by emphasizing certain matters within the Christian tradition, not by going outside it. If one has the experience of the living Christ, this is inevitable. This is why, sadly, I have to part company with the liberal Quakers, mainly of the unprogrammed tradition, who regard these things as being only of historical interest unless re-interpreted in a different mode.

The finality of Christ is expressed in John's Gospel, where Jesus says to Philip, "...he who has seen me has seen the Father." The two most enduring images of God the Christian religion offers are a homeless baby among the animals in an outhouse, and a crucified carpenter. They are the best answer a Christian can give to the question, what is God like? These images are truths of faith, and nobody has ever reasoned their way to belief in them. They protect the truth from the wise and make it accessible to the simple-minded and simple hearted. They come from the topsy-turvy kingdom.

If we hear the hidden call these images make, we find it necessary to draw near and see how these strange things came to happen. Then we are embraced by a mystery which says that here is the deepest symbol for the activity of the divine in the created world, and here also are events which actually took place in the harsh and unforgiving world of solid reality. The story of Jesus

Christ may enthrall us because it is a myth in the fullest sense of that word, but it also binds us because it is simply, factually, true.

We can leave on one side all that follows in Christian doctrine from these things. We are concerned with those of other faiths who are not touched by this recitation. It is sufficient to remark that the very ordinariness of Jesus, his response to the violence that was offered him, and the conviction that he had thereby conquered death led his first followers to the point where they could only express what they had experienced of him by saying that he was God.

So many people overlook the stupendous consequences of this, looking for God in Jesus rather than for Christ in God. If, truly, Christ Jesus and the Father are one, there is not one person on this planet, who, invoking the deity by whatever name they know, is not calling on the God whom Christians worship in Christ. Here is the Quaker doctrine of the light, approached in another way. The pearl, the mustard seed, the light is planted in all people and is a sufficient guide to life if heeded in humility and sincerity. This is why the unprogrammed meeting, barren of images, innocent of words, is a place where those of true faith can come together to worship.

Here we approach the kernel of relations between the faiths. There is a kind of witness to Christ among the nations which requires treachery. This particular call to conversion is destructive of family, upbringing, language, customs, tradition and lively faith in God. It knows little of fulfillment and seeks an outward conformity with the letter.

There is another witness which places the challenge of the gospel before the world, not the written record of it. The Christ within all is no different from the Christ of history—except that he is alive and often incognito. The challenge of his gospel is to turn and change, to embrace self-denial, simplicity and servanthood, to hear the call to obedience and righteousness. Wherever this call is heard, under whatever name, there is a confirmation of the passion and resurrection of Christ, and there is salvation.

Starting
to
Worship
Without
Words

First
Steps
in the
Silence

People give many reasons for going to unprogrammed meetings, some good, some not really satisfactory, but the opportunity for prolonged and undisturbed prayer seems to me to be the best. I won't quarrel about what the definition of prayer is. My way is not everybody's. But a Friends meeting that is not based upon a deep faith that God can be encountered in the heart, and that we can enjoy a heartfelt, divine communion in one another's company is not a Friends meeting, whatever else it may be. Prayer is the encounter with God in the heart, and the traditional fivefold division of the ways of that encounter do not seem to me ever to have been bettered.

At the same time, the ways to God are many, and we have to discover most of them on our own. They appear when we are ready for them and when our faithfulness has shown we can live with the consequences of further growth. This is one of the most important parts of Quaker spirituality, but I was not told anything about that when I first began to go to meeting. My presence was noted by the overseers I now know, but I was left entirely on my own, and I am thankful that I was. I was busy learning to pray, and that was sufficient. Like so many learners, I thought I was doing it myself. In the fulness of time I realised that it was God who was leading me on.

If I were to be asked, therefore, what advice I would give to a newcomer to unprogrammed or semi-programmed Quaker meetings, I would echo Paul's words to the Thessalonians, "Pray without ceasing." I would add that it is necessary to develop one's prayer life in new ways. What follows is intended to be helpful to Friends and those who come to meeting fairly often without necessarily becoming members of the Society. It may also be of interest to others, but it is not an authoritative statement of how to do it. There can be no such thing; the whole point of Quaker worship is that we find our own way.

To some people, prayer comes easily. Others have to toil at it. Most people find they have periods of ease and difficulty alternately. The best thing to do if you want to make progress in prayer is exactly what you would do if you decided to take up tennis or golf—find a coach. Golf and tennis pros cannot play your game for you, but the wealth of their experience is at your disposal.

To have a spiritual friend is an ancient tradition which is being revived in our time. When I was beginning on my journey I did not have this privilege, but now I have such people. Prayer is the art of being, not doing, and what you learn from your friend is not how to pray by numbers, but by feelings and attitudes and responses. Spiritual friends are not really coaches but partners in growth. It is simple to start such a relationship. You invite someone willing, whose spiritual life you are happy with, to meet you regularly for a period of worship and prayer in which you can lay before that person, and discuss, what you feel is happening to you in your life.

The next piece of advice is practical. Do not expect to sit for an hour and have godly thoughts all the time. That would be more than flesh could stand. You should expect to give some consideration to the files waiting for you in the office on Monday, to think about the bonfire you are planning to build when you get home, to worry whether you left the garage doors open, to wonder what reason your children have to be so objectionable and inconsiderate. Learn to accept these things, for they are part of the life you are offering to God.

In your own way you will come back to your prayer and then wander again. Sometimes your prayer will be quite long, at other times brief. Unless you are a highly organised person you won't have any kind of order. It may help to begin with a sort of mental agenda, ticking things off as you go, but you may well find, if you can forget any guilt feelings about your wandering attention, that after a few meetings, you will not need to be so highly organised. If you have a proper period of prayer every day, you will be able to be ever freer on First Days.

And now I must be honest and admit to much of what I actually do in meeting. Certainly I pray and meditate, but I also do many other things. I daydream, I sing silently or hum inaudible tunes. On occasion I have gone to sleep, so I suppose slumber would be one of my meeting activities. I carry a little Bible in my jacket pocket, and though it is for reference, I must own up to reading it. There are other things Friends read, but that is my bag.

I often get bored. I fidget. I have to cope with my own body and its periodic discomfort. I shut my eyes and then open them and then shut them again for no very good reason. I wonder whether X wears a wig or what brand of toothpaste Y prefers or whatever induced K and L to marry. I think about work, about other people, about personal problems and relationships. I grumble a bit to myself, since I talk to myself a lot anyway. I periodically attempt to clear my mind, but much of the time I simply think. I speculate about theology but usually manage to make it subservient to my worship. I also think about the government and the state of the world, and I make it a principle to give serious and sympathetic consideration to all the spoken ministry.

So beginners and visitors to Friends meetings who are unaccustomed to the silence need to realise that the Quakers are doing just what they are doing. There is no secret way of coping with silence. You just get on with it. I do not wish to leave the impression that this is all there is, though. That would be very far from the truth. But we do not need to enter murky theological waters, we need simply to register that if meeting were nothing more than sitting in silence having pleasant but wandering thoughts, Quaker worship would be a wool-gathering farce.

While stressing that the actual experience of passing time in a Friends meeting is likely to be similar between newcomer and old hand, we must also acknowledge that there is much that one can learn about the practise of this kind of worship. There are more effective and less effective ways of coming to meeting. What makes for equality is that the effective ones are not habit forming. An experienced Friend will know them, and how to explain them to others. But only what the Catholic tradition knows as an act of will permits their exercise. God adds spice to Quaker life by ensuring that the less effective ways *are* habit forming and can be a snare for the soul. Once adopted, Quaker worship can be dangerous. Its characteristic sin is complacency.

The following observations are intended to help and reassure anyone who may be thinking about a visit to an unprogrammed meeting, or who is uneasy at the thought that more earth-shattering experiences ought to be coming their way and aren't. The situation is normal and calls for nothing more than patience and a bit of common sense. These are some of the things I have found.

There are people who are secret members of the hair shirt brigade. A hair shirt was a scratchy garment particularly holy people were supposed to have worn in the Middle Ages to mortify the flesh and benefit the soul. I bet all it did was to make them bad tempered and objectionable. The modern hair shirt brigade thinks that you can only worship properly if you are cold and uncomfortable. So meeting houses must have cold water flowing from the hot taps, damp towels, hard benches and draughts. Do not attend such places. Go where you can sit comfortably. This is very important. You are not there for the self-control Olympics, you are there to worship God in the beauty of holiness, and the best way to be still is to be comfortable.

When you have found a relaxing posture that you can keep for a while, remember it. Find others, and consciously adopt them throughout the period of the meeting. For example, you may like to fold your hands on your lap at one point. At another you might like to have them open, palms up, resting on your thighs. This can help your meditations too. Open hands are open to God, who will fill them with grace. They are open to the world, a sign of trust and strength. A bowed head or a straight head can express unconscious movement or can be used to express a mood of worship. Many meeting houses have hassocks. Time was, quite recently, that Friends used them to kneel on to pray. That is a better use than a lodging for dirty boots.

Since everyday distractions are at a minimum in an unprogrammed meeting, one becomes conscious of all sort of things that are usually beneath our regular attention, like a hole in a tooth, a shaving cut, a leaky shoe, ill-fitting underwear, fat where there wasn't fat before. Usually we feel such things and then dismiss them until we get home and can put them right. But at meeting, we are stuck for a pretty long time, and our body keeps protesting that it wants our urgent and undivided attention, even though we have given it warmth and comfort. It must be ignored gently. The best way to accomplish this is constant deep breathing, relaxed and regular, all the way from the solar plexus, on and on till the regularity of it takes you over, as most times it surely will.

Friends have different preferences about closing their eyes, as can be seen by glancing round the meeting house. I have difficulty if I close mine too soon, but I find that with deep, regular breathing, the surface distractions diminish and closing my eyes helps to accelerate this process. Somehow the power of silence becomes tangible at this point. After a few minutes of stillness I may have the sensation that my mental powers are being concentrated as a bird wraps itself in it wings and that I am coming into harmony with the other worshippers. This is the process known as 'centering down'.

This can be done far more effectively if one has come, to use another Quaker phrase, with heart and mind prepared. The hint about breathing is based on the experience that regularity and order, or perhaps rhythm, are as essential to silent worship as they are to other things. To come rushed and untidy to the meeting house at any other time than an emergency is to break all the organic links between our lives outside worship and our meeting. The silence is then a refuge and not a reflection of what we seek to practise every day. Whenever I go to meeting full of turmoil, centering down is like ploughing a rocky, stony field.

Underlying this advice is a conviction about how we ought to live. We are conscious of time and depth in our lives in all sorts of ways. In modern society we tend to live at speed, trying to do all manner of things, and often to do them simultaneously. Moreover we live in a world of almost instant visual and aural gratification, and we move very fast from one object of attention to another. That is how work, transportation, TV and the media of communication organise things for us. So a Friends meeting has these strikes against it when it invites us to search for God's time and God's depth in our lives and refuses to compromise with the habits formed by the timetable and the calendar. During the week we need to try to take things one at a time and more slowly. The quality of worship improves that way.

There are Friends who think that we should clear our minds of everything when we come to meeting, that preparation is some sort of obstacle to the proper use of silence, and that we should rely on something happening to us after the meeting has been going a little while. I doubt whether that is good advice. To succeed in something as demanding as silent worship and to come to the point at which one can treat the silence in this way needs a great deal of experience. So as part of one's private worship during the week before attending meeting, one should look out for a thought, a text, a theme, or an idea on which to work, and which will complement or expand one's prayer.

One of the troubles everybody experiences occasionally is the inability to focus the mind. When I am in this mood there seems no getting out of it. Sometimes I am unable to concentrate on worship at all. At other times thoughts wander persistently and my mind seldom stays still for more than a few moments. At other times I am intensely disturbed by something I usually do not notice, like the ticking of the clock, or a cough, or the coins rattling in somebody else's pocket.

The problem here is usually frustration that I am failing to achieve what I came for and guilt that I ought to be using the time better. Hard though it was, I had to learn that neither of these things matters. Two things help. In my mind, I have learned to recognise my guilt and frustration and to set them on one side and look at them. Their power diminishes if I do that. Then I am able to feel better about the problem of maintaining concentration by using this little stratagem for bringing a wandering mind back to its path.

I try to come to meeting with a word, a phrase, a text, something memorable or important, in case I need it. I have a little stock of things like prayers or memories of places. When my mind wanders, I repeat my text or review my memory as often as it takes to restore concentration. This is the discipline of the silence. Learning the art of concentration is to learn that God's time and God's depth are here in the meeting, but they have a price.

Another feature of the way we live now which affects our worship is that we are educated to think at the expense of knowing how to feel. I do not for a moment wish to undervalue thought or to advocate a self-indulgent emotionalism. But many people would agree that we have got the balance wrong. Our emotions and our sensitivity need to be trained and developed too. Our knowledge of our selves and our capacity to respond to God and God's creation can only be enhanced thereby.

Yet the advice to come with a thought, text, theme or idea needs qualification. Another difficulty we have to learn to handle is that some meetings are wasted because we do not understand the mood in which we come, and we attempt to pray and meditate in a fashion quite alien to our underlying feelings. This is part of the secret of good self-examination. This is not a process of self-criticism so much as self-discernment. Its aim is to strengthen us, and this is one of the ways in which it can.

One of the things I do during the week in preparation for meeting is to ask myself what I need. This is part of the austerity of life which I have described. I have to come to terms with things in my life which I would rather ignore. Sometimes I am not well. I need healing. I know there is not going to be a miracle, but my mood will be one of patience and expectation, and much of my time in meeting will be spent in this exercise.

It may be that I have a problem of some sort, not necessarily of world-shattering importance. I seek understanding, relief of my puzzlement. Or I have felt far from God, spiritually lonely. So I will come needing God's company and simply sit, enjoying it. Naturally, the beauty of life also inspires this kind of mood-devotion. There are moods of joy, repose, curiosity, challenge, well-being, humour, memory, hopefulness. The list is endless. It contains as many items as the shades of feeling and sentiment that we have. The dominant ones make up our personality. They are our strength. So to find them and use them in worship is one of the most creative things we can do. That is another of the ways in which the silence works change.

Underlying this way of worship is a conviction about God. It is that our relationship with the divine is formed at many different levels and is experienced at many different intensities. Consider your relationship with somebody you love deeply. You will have attitudes and values in common with that person, but points of quite radical difference. You will have a pattern of giving and receiving and of forbearance and encouragement in response to one another's needs. Your loving will sometimes be easy, sometimes hard, sometimes put into words, sometimes sensed or signalled according to some private code that only you understand. You are careful and reckless in turn. You do things you are ashamed of and things that make you proud. A growing relationship is changing. It is alive. It has many, many different aspects. So it is with worship. A one-dimensional relationship with God is a sure sign of spiritual immaturity.

So it is important to stress this non-intentional, non-intellectual kind of worship. The great liturgical tradition of Christianity is built up of innumerable words and phrases. But to see it primarily in verbal terms is to miss the point. A bird on the wing has no thought for what it is doing. Flight is a flowing unity, not the cobbling together of thousands of separate actions. So it is with worship. We engage our emotions, our moods, our sensations and bring before God the whole rhythm and texture of our lives. On the surface the Quaker meeting may look as if it stands at one end of the tradition of Christian worship, but under the surface the silence is giving form to life. It is moulding us into the people God wants us to be and pointing our faces towards heaven.

Symbols
and
Images

In some ways the art of worship is about the making of images. In Catholic or Orthodox churches there are statues, paintings and music, incense, costume and glass, all contrived with the architecture itself to impress the senses of the worshippers and to enhance their sense of divine glory and eternal truth. There are the mosaics in the Byzantine apses, the intimate statues of virgin and child in medieval gothic lady-chapels, the towers and the bells, the ikons and the crucifixes, and above all, the singing, the water, the bread and the wine. God is not in the images, but the way towards God is through them.

Though on the surface it looks totally dissimilar, the Society of Friends has affinities with this tradition, for the art of silent worship was brought to a peak of perfection in the monastic communities that cultivated the Quaker values long before there were any Quakers. So if we put historical and theological considerations on one side and look into the heart of worship, we can begin to uncover what these affinities are.

Consider the irony for those of us who see ourselves as Protestants. We are a step removed from the great musical and pictorial tradition of European culture. We may sing hymns (though not often, if we are Quakers of the unprogrammed tradition) and the occasional oratorio. We may own reproductions of pictures that have a religious significance for us, but the mass we possess is given in the concert hall. The pieta, the Virgin, the crucifixion we experience in the bright neutrality of the picture gallery.

It needs an effort of will, sometimes, to remember these things were created for the church, and that is where they still belong. They came into being because they were the best offering that those who made them or commissioned them could give to God. The surface contrast with silent contemplation could not be sharper. But we need to remember that silent prayer in earlier Christianity was always firmly rooted in monastic routines and the eucharist as the ultimate sign of the church. In the Society of Friends, on the other hand, the silent meeting stands alone and bears the full symbolic weight of the values, faith and practise of the Quakers. Is there any way in which the freely adopted discipline of worshipping God without any outward aids can nevertheless show a comparison?

The importance of a silent Quaker meeting lies in its total emptiness. Quakerism began as a movement of renewal in the church, but a turbulent, provocative and challenging kind of renewal. So intense was the inward spiritual experience this renewal offered that the symbolic system it inherited seemed lifeless, and Friends discarded it. The silence is less significant for what it is than what it is not. It marks a protest against clothing an inward faith in rich outward garments and entertaining it with music, song, and eloquence and dignity.

Friends saw dangers in such signs and symbols and considered that those who remained devoted to them were wedded to the old ways and lived in the letter rather than the life. Even among Friends there would be a tendency to fall back into the outwardness of religion, so all outward representation had to be avoided—not only church ornaments and vestments but visible liturgy, congregational singing and observation of the great festivals. Early Quakers even denied that there was a sabbath day in the new dispensation. Their symbolism was in fact very rich, but it was solely inward, solely spiritual and solely biblical.

Leaving historical and theological considerations on one side, we can see that Quakerism of the old style was an elaborate technique for avoiding idolatry, evidently one of the early Quakers' major spiritual concerns. Ironically, this protest against all outward symbols actually created another one, the anti-symbol of silence, for, in fact, we cannot escape from symbolism.

What matters is the sort of symbols we have. Religious symbols are neutral in themselves, but human beings have the capacity to turn them at will into ikons or idols. If we are aware of the power of idols, we have a chance of protecting ourselves from their power and are better able to recognise the promptings of the Holy Spirit within.

Ikons and idols can have a physical shape, but they are actually symbols in the mind. They stand at opposite ends of the spectrum. An ikon is so close to the divine truth it represents that the worshipper can see right through it. It becomes, so to speak, invisible, for it shows us God. An idol draws our attention away from divine truth by substituting the plausible and acceptable for the challenging and transforming.

We all work with images because we have a pictorial way of thinking. In religion our images can go one way or the other. We can use a spiritual discipline to make ikons of them, or we can allow them to degenerate into idols. Originally, Friends were so afraid of the latter course that they tried to root all outward symbolism out of their religious lives. Looking back, we can see the dangers in this and may not wish to follow them, but in fact their instincts were sound. This was the only way they had of making sure that their practise matched their profession.

It is likely that most of us today will be aware of the importance of symbolism in our lives and appreciate rather better the way in which imagery is essential to our ability to cope successfully with the demands the world makes on us. The power of myth is often the key to understanding. Notwithstanding the fact that they can be manipulated and debased, the literary and visual arts can be among the most ennobling influences on our lives.

Thus, if we regard worship as an art, and the great corpus of religious music and painting as branches of it, we have a way of seeing silent worship that makes better and more modern sense. In the Quaker meeting and the hermit's cell, a skill is being practised, a vision seen, a voice heard, an offering held up to God. It is no less real for being invisible. It is no less important because it is seen only by God. It is no less of an achievement because there is no formal training to be had in it. Its substance is the self-expression of the individual soul to God to the fullest possible degree. Silent worship is an art and, in common with all the arts, it involves a skill which can be learned.

That is not to claim that one can learn a few techniques and pass oneself off as an artist in prayer, as if all one needs is to know a few tricks or dodges, how to string a few prayers together or what sort of meditation to adopt. What makes an artist is not so much skill as the way it is used and the purpose to which it is put.

Certainly one cannot produce prayer to order. But within oneself, silent worship creates an ability to recognise and organise one's strengths and weaknesses and to dispose the soul to meet the requirements both God and the world place upon it. It helps us to deal with novelties and challenges and to turn them to good account. It gives us self-confidence in what we are doing. Without that, it is almost impossible to acquire a skill in anything.

Plainly there is also a medium. Art is creative activity expressed through some medium. The artist can choose wood or stone, paint or metal, words or instruments, conceivably film cameras and prime time on TV. Artists can even use computers or strobe lights. Having got the medium together, they do their thing. It does not really matter whether there is a creative urge or whether they seek to interpret somebody else, the effect is the same. They get on with it. In our case, the silence is the medium in which things are made and in which the skill of creating prayer is nurtured.

Apart from the occasional crew of iconoclasts, nobody really believes that art can be random or anarchic. If the need for some sort of skill is part of its definition, that has to be so. Skill, however, is not possessed in a vacuum. It is always latent until put to use. Hence there has to be an intention in making a work of art, something you wish to achieve, a purpose. As we have already seen, an hour of silence presents all kinds of possibilities, all kinds of challenges. Which we choose to take up will depend on what our immediate spiritual needs are. But our freedom of response must be tempered by a longer view. Our conscious purposes give a framework to our particular meeting experiences, and we should try not to worship hand to mouth.

The last feature of art that we must recognise is that artists are always defeated either by the limitations of their vision or by the medium itself. There is no way to replicate reality. We are ultimately going to be frustrated if we try, for, at the deepest level, this is trespassing on holy ground, presuming on God. Certainly we can gain deep insight into aspects of reality by our art, for interpretation is a continual process of uncovering the possibilities inherent in the world. But what we cannot do is to produce a synoptic vision that will adequately express the glory we know. If we are to avoid a corroding frustration, we have to learn a resignation of spirit when we have given what we can and simply accept what is. In the art of prayer this resignation is called reverence—the admission of our creatureliness.

If this is true, those of us who worship in the unprogrammed tradition should be able to recognise its counterpart in the liturgical tradition. As the communities of the past created sanctuaries of great outward glory, the Religious Society of Friends provides in its silent meetings the opportunity for each worshipper to create his or her own sanctuary of inward glory. This is another of those reasons why many modern Friends are surprised to discover who their soul-friends really are. If the outward signs of the Christian faith draw their meaning from the mystery within, that mystery can only be experienced when the language of symbolism has been mastered. For some, those symbols must be in the fabric of the outside world. For others, the symbols need to be within the soul. But the need is the same. Symbols there must be, and we have to work to possess them.

Let us look now at what it is we are seeking to express in our worship. The word itself is pretty hard to define, and dictionaries are seldom much help. Whenever I look something up, I get trapped on a roundabout of definitions. One word is explained by reference to another one, and when I look that up, I often find myself back at the word I started with. I end up with a collection of words all defined in terms of one another, and I am never much the wiser.

If we start with the question, "What is worship?" and run to some authoritative source like a dictionary, then we shall not get a very serviceable answer. But if we say, "What are the thoughts and experiences that we ought to call worship?" and then go on and reflect upon our own lives, we might see more clearly. We should start at the beginning, with ourselves, for the first stage in all creative worship is to realise that in coming to God we do not deny ourselves, we reach our fulfillment. It is our coming into the light.

On the surface, this might appear to contradict the teaching of Jesus that we can only become his disciples through self-denial, but it is not really so. God says to us through Jeremiah, "Before I formed you in the womb I knew you." We are not clones, the by-products of an experiment or a process designed to do something else. We are here, each one of us, by divine grace and intention, and it is divine love that brought us into being. John writes in his first letter, "We love him because he first loved us." So to worship, it is essential for us to come to the knowledge that we are each very dear to God.

There is no other starting point. We need this absolute security before we can practise the sort of self-denial Jesus was talking about. Self-denigration is sterile to the individual and an insult to God. But as we give our selves willingly to God, in love, God's own self-sacrificing love floods in, and we become children of the light. Worship is therefore not the order of service in a church, nor devotion, homage or reverence. Those can become worship, to be sure, but they are not its essence. Worship is being touched and loved by God, coming into a relationship that is sometimes pretty stormy and is never dull.

Worship means opening the heart, and Quakers will say that silent meeting for worship is one of the very best places where this can happen. Words, symbols and thoughts can pull away the briars, cobwebs and old planks that obstruct and clutter up the doorway of the heart, but when the door itself swings open, we leave them all at the threshold. It is then we enter the real sanctuary, and the silence comes alive.

This is the turning point in the religious life that we all have to come to in our own way. Images spring to mind. We may be said to discover the brook flowing in our hearts. We may feel ourselves embraced by the wind of the Spirit. There is a Quaker way of getting here, and other ways in other traditions. But what happens is the same. Those who have had this experience speak of becoming their true selves. They are given a perspective on the world that comes from beyond it.

In Quaker parlance this is called coming to the light, and it has a dimension of intense ethical and spiritual struggle. That of God which is called the 'light' is positive, powerful and active. It speaks to us and leads us, and therefore the appropriate attitudes for us to take are of waiting and listening for it. These are not at the outset passive attitudes, but are rather the moods in which one's prayer or self-examination take place. The point is that we try to make ourselves receptive to God.

It must also be remembered that Friends have never regarded this as an individual activity. People who regard Friends meetings as opportunities for meditation have failed to appreciate this corporate aspect. The waiting and listening are activities in which everybody is engaged and, as we shall see, produce spoken ministry which helps to articulate the common guidance which the Holy Spirit is believed to give the group as a whole. So the waiting and listening is corporate also. This is why Friends emphasize the 'ministry of silence' and the importance of coming to meeting regularly and with heart and mind prepared. The similarities with liturgy continue to reveal themselves.

Different writers about Quakerism, not all Friends, arrive at different estimates of silence. Perhaps it has different levels. So far, I have been regarding it primarily as a *medium*, that through which one does something; for people learning to worship after the manner of Friends, that may be the most helpful way of understanding it.

Others, however, almost make silence an *object*, a thing to be experienced and taken on its own terms. The point here is that we accommodate ourselves to the absence of sound and allow it to mould our spiritual experiences. This has (to some) the advantage of doing away with the necessity of a specifically Christian spirituality and permitting other kinds of belief to take a place within the overall pattern of Quaker worship. Indeed, belief may be irrelevant. The experience of silence itself may somehow refresh us, revive us, revitalise us, and return us renewed into the world for whatever it is we have to do there.

Then there are those who see silence as a *sign* or *symbol*. This is where the silent Friends in the world would take theological issue with those who have programmed worship services. On the basis of a church order which refuses ordained ministry and outward expression of baptism or the supper and which places the highest practical value on waiting for direct divine leadings, the silence actually proclaims the tradition, because no other practise is possible within it. To participate in the silence, for those Friends, is to be a Quaker.

So it is possible to think of silence in several ways and thereby gain a valuable perspective on what we are doing. Often, reflection will show that we have a preference or a bias for one or the other aspect of silence. That is a considerable advantage, for we can use that knowledge in our preparations and for worship itself.

We will then be more able to encounter the problems of silence with confidence, aware that the best way to use it is our own way. We all have to learn to make space for ourselves where we can simply be and cut ourselves off from everything else. We shall need to discover the particular rhythm of thought and rest in the silence that is agreeable to us. We need to experiment to find out and to practice and work at our prayer and meditation.

Most silent meetings last for an hour, so we also have to learn that gift which is equally important to tennis players, stand-up comics and Quakers of the unprogrammed tradition—timing. We can put it this way. The silent meeting is like the surface of a lake. We enter it in our devotions and begin to sink into its depths. On rare occasions we rise again to the sunlight of everyday life when the whole meeting ends, and there is a sense of perfection, of completion. Sometimes, as I did on my first meeting, we finish before the meeting ends and just have to sit there, well-manneredly waiting for everybody else.

At other times the reverse happens, and we are not ready to finish our worship when the official closure comes. Moreover, we soon make the acquaintance of two disappointments—the meeting in which we totally fail to worship and flit about on the surface of the silence, unable to break into it, and the meeting in which we are unable to achieve any depth at all and paddle in and out of the silence, frustrated because we know what we are missing.

As the shape of the silent meeting and the ways we can approach it begin to emerge, we begin to learn the discipline of structuring our worship over time. If we think about what we actually do, we can begin to find possibilities for ourselves, and, thence, lines of growth. By thinking about the times when we reach depths of worship, we can make ourselves more open to receive this blessing. By preparing properly and by learning how to concentrate better, we can minimise the difficulties which, in fact, we never entirely overcome. Finally, when a meeting is not going well for us, there are things we can do even then to turn it to good account.

This is where we can discover that worship is an art. Amateurs, by definition, can go and do something else when the going gets hard. That is why they very rarely excel. Professionals have the hard-won knowledge that when difficulty comes, their craft will take them through. It is as if an energy from outside takes over and raises what they do to a higher power in one act of transformation. If we are willing, this is what God can do with our worship.

Listening
to
Ministry

I have been sitting in Friends meetings for about thirty years now, and I must say I remember very little of the ministry I have heard during that time. That is as it should be, for the function of ministry is the spiritual formation of Friends, not their instruction.

One of the most memorable pieces of ministry I ever heard was given by an elderly Friend shortly after I first came into membership of the Society. He rose and stood in his characteristically stooped way, with his finger in his little pocket Bible, and said that we ought all to be picking up sticks. I sat up in surprise at this, and then heard him tell the story of Elijah going to the widow of Zarephath for refuge, and how he had found her gathering fuel for a fire on which she would probably never have anything to cook.

I thought he was crazy. He must have drawn a moral from this, but I do not remember what it was. Much later, however, as I began to reflect on the nature of Quaker ministry, it became clear to me. This message operated at two levels. There was certainly an element of teaching in it. The Old Testament was being applied to modern life, and I was being pointed to it in no uncertain terms. There was also an element of exhortation. He said that we ought to pick up sticks too.

That was why I thought he was touched. As a new Quaker I didn't want this kind of puzzle, I wanted grand visions, inspirational sermons, endorsement of all the things I brought to the Society of Friends in my youthful enthusiasm. I now realise that I did not want to be ministered to; I wanted a message. I wanted something to enjoy or react to, something I could deal with, take to bits, pack up for future reference or throw away as useless or unacceptable. I listened with my mind, not my heart, and I did not hear what was being said.

Nevertheless, by the grace of God, my elderly Friend's words lodged in my mind. I have always remembered them. I never quite appreciated why, until, having gone through a number of changes over the years, I began to see traditional Quaker spirituality as a living option for my own life. The sticks the widow was gathering were collected in faith, with no clear idea of their ultimate use. Faith and habit were carrying her on. But she had more than sticks. Put together they were something else again—fire, one of the most powerful and frightening things in human experience.

Thus it is in the world of the Spirit, my old ministering Friend was saying. Having a good trip in this meeting is all very well, but you must take a longer view. If you garner all the gifts of imagination and reflection which God sends you, you will have something which can catch fire. But like the widow, you must be faithful and patient.

The next piece of memorable ministry did rise out of my faithfulness, in a funny way. On another occasion, soon after I was married, there had been a snowstorm. My wife and I knew that many people would be prevented from coming to meeting, so we felt under a special obligation to struggle through the drifts to get to the meeting house, which was in the forest. When we arrived we found chairs set out in a small side room in front of a large coke fire which filled the fireplace, burned brightly, but made almost no impact on the arctic temperature in the room.

During meeting we received ministry from another elderly Friend who was bright of eye, sharp of nose and wit, and who always wore a broad-brimmed hat tied under her chin with a wide black ribbon. In her precise voice she pointed out how Britain believes that snow is un-British and consequently never takes sensible precautions against it, simply wishing it would go away. She was right. British people on the whole think it is bad mannered of the weather to snow, and that was how we came to be a little band of survivors, huddled together for warmth, worshipping in conditions of some discomfort, affronted at climatic bad form.

Our Friend then changed gear and drew our attention to the prodigious range of temperatures in the universe and how narrow, in fact, was the band in which we lived, where it took a drop of only about twenty degrees to snarl up so much of our normal pattern of life. If it were to stay like this, she told us, there would be no spring and no harvest, and when the cans of beans ran out, that would be it.

That piece of ministry has also stayed with me for many years. I was at a time of life and in a period (the sixties) when there was unbridled optimism abroad. We could do *anything*, particularly if we were young. But the snow that day put a question mark against some of my assumptions, particularly my values in worship. As I have said, I did much thinking by my own strength in those days. Our dear Friend's ministry probably marked the beginning of my understanding of what reverence meant and that intimacy with God does not mean familiarity. There are things we are not meant to know, or to do, and we have to learn what they are. They are God's and they are holy.

Perhaps the third piece of ministry which I remember vividly was from a Friend more of my own generation, a man of spiritual weight, with a dry and magnificent sense of humour. I once heard him remark that things are not what they were, with the Catholics having doubts and the Quakers getting short of money. He rose once, about the turn of the year and quoted, I guess, Ezekiel, who says, (3:16) "Son of Man, I have made you a watchman for the house of Israel..." He described how he chose for each year a role, as it were, to explore in his own devotional life. This year it was to be the role of watchman. Standing in Ezekiel's shoes, what did God have to say to him?

I have not followed his example as an annual discipline, but his words have been very important to me at different times in my life. I have found that when I am going through particular periods of stress or change, I look for some such model and explore it. I have found that it works like a radio receiver. You are on a wave band, and you can pick up all sorts of messages that are always there, but you usually don't either notice or need. I have found this a great aid in spiritual discernment for myself. What arises in another's ministry often falls like seed in one's own life, and the discipline of waiting in silence gives time for germination and for this process of discernment.

Discernment is a fashionable word in religious circles these days, but it is really no big deal. In ordinary life, it is simply the ability to distinguish, or separate things out. It is like choosing things, or naming them, and is a closely related activity. Indeed, it is basic to both. In principle, spiritual discernment is no different. It is the activity of the soul in deepening its relationship with God.

That may involve many things, but its most obvious application in Quaker life is in the process of weighing the words given in ministry at the meeting for worship. No sooner do we sit down in an unprogrammed meeting than the questions are put before us—how do we recognise genuine ministry when we hear it, and how do we recognise our own call to minister when it comes? Many newcomers are likely to be too busy exploring the nature of an unfamiliar way of worshipping to pay much attention to these matters, but the time comes when they cannot be avoided.

It has to be admitted right at the start that not all ministry is equally helpful, or that we should take it at face value just because it is given in a meeting for worship. There is trivial as well as profound ministry. It can arise from deep experience but sometimes seems to express only personal whim. Mostly it will answer to the spiritual needs of the meeting, but it can sometimes be seen to have no value beyond expressing the immediate need of the person who gives it. So part of the art of spiritual discernment in an unprogrammed meeting is to decide how to respond to ministry when we have heard it.

First there is the courtesy we should expect to extend to any deeply felt expression of feeling or opinion. What matters is what is said, not the way it is put. Hence we have to make conscious efforts not to be impressed by eloquence or to judge people from outward appearances. The simple can frequently see further into the nature of things than those wise in the ways of the world. People may have annoying mannerisms, and we must be careful to ignore them.

Again, it helps to be able to interpret what kind of ministry is being given. In the old days, they expected prayer, praise and preaching. There is a lot more than that nowadays, though, on reflection, most offerings can be made to fall into one or other of those categories. Some Friends speak earnestly, exhorting the meeting and often sharpening up its moral or spiritual sensitivity in disconcerting ways. Others get up and chat, almost absent-mindedly, but may produce a profound insight, like a gift of diamonds wrapped up in newspaper. Some ministers sound a trumpet call to action in the world. Some play a reed pipe, pointing the worshippers to the hidden currents of divine activity deep below the surface of life.

Though it might not be obvious on the surface, ministry should be coherent and structured and given for a purpose. Since the urge to speak often comes welling up from a deep place, this order may not be fully grasped by the Friend speaking and may acquire shape as it is expressed. So we have to help it along by sympathetic understanding and imagination and try to be sensitive to what the minister is striving to say.

This is why style must be taken into consideration. The old Quakers thought ministry was being a sort of flute for the Holy Spirit to play on. You had to be quite passive and let God do the talking through you. This view is still to be found, but most modern Friends in the unprogrammed tradition put it rather differently. Since we are created with differences of temperament and insight, we may expect to be given different gifts to be used, each in our own way.

It follows, I think, that we have to train ourselves to overcome our personal likes and dislikes and treat everything said in meeting with uniform seriousness and consideration. That is part of Friends' spiritual discipline and cannot be compromised with. It is not at all easy, but it is unavoidable. If we are to practise discernment we have to do it at a spiritual and not a merely intellectual level. We need time and calmness to reflect on what we have heard. Only when we have taken it into ourselves shall we be in a position to decide whether or not it is from God.

The ministry given in the silence of unprogrammed meetings and in the open worship of programmed meetings is thus of unique importance in Quakerism. When our personal response harmonises with what is said at a level below everyday preoccupations and prejudices, the ministry will be sound. But if it fails this test, we have to let it 'go over us'. The price of discrimination is that we receive the words tenderly but cannot accept them as a prophetic utterance.

There is a celebrated passage from the *Journal* of George Fox which is part of a letter written by him to Friends in the ministry.

Many Friends know it by heart. It goes, "Be patterns, be examples in all countries, places, islands, nations, wherever you come, that your carriage and life may preach among all sorts of people, and to them; then you will come to walk cheerfully over the world, answering that of God in every one." The art of discerning the value of ministry in a silent meeting for worship is to test whether what is said reaches, or answers, that of God within you.

Where these two things meet, the ministry has been given genuinely, or 'in the life'. The revelation of truth which God imparts to you in the depth of your own soul receives and confirms what has been said by the person to whom the words have been given. There is no escaping the consequences of this. The early Quakers took it to be the experience of the first Christians and what underlies the passages in the New Testament about the early church and its worship.

Listening to ministry is part of the art of spiritual discernment, so it makes sense to think about the manner of its delivery as well as its content. Though this is not perhaps one of the main purposes in developing our capacity to hear, long experience of the ministry of others can teach us that we have the capacity to minister ourselves. God often teaches us to recognise his personal call to us by giving us a sympathetic understanding of his call to other people. If we can understand the different ways ministry comes to us, we shall learn how we may ourselves be moved to minister.

Years before I spoke my first words in meeting, I had the longing to minister. It was not a dishonourable desire arising from my own conceit. Many of the ministers I heard were able to see the hand of God at work in everyday life in a way that was denied to me at that time. Rather it was the wish to have that gift of practical wisdom out of which I knew ministry grew. As my ministry drew near, I began to notice how different Friends approached their ministry in different ways, but how there was an underlying pattern.

Looking back I think I can remember certain stages in my journey towards this particular call. I know for sure that it took a very long time, and I remember being quite fretful that I, always pretty eloquent, was given no words. Looking back, I know that this was God dealing with me. I have come to learn that our faithfulness is always tested in our willingness to set aside those things we value most—particularly the personal qualities in which we have every reason to feel ourselves blessed. This is so we can know that when they are ready for use, they are being put to God's purposes, not our own.

If I had to draw a chart, or name stages, I should say that after a while it dawned on me that there was a possibility that I might one day minister. I was too busy learning silent worship, so I did not consider it at length. But after a while the notion returned, this time arousing in me an inclination. This was something I was equipped to do, so why not do it? But this time I knew the difference between speech and ministry, so I could answer myself. But the next time the leading returned, it had changed into a desire.

This stayed with me for some years, and then, shortly before I first spoke, the tempo changed rapidly. The cloak of desire was thrown aside and intention appeared. I knew it was only a matter of time. I was going to minister. Then I felt the need to minister, as if I was carrying a burden. Then, on that fresh December day, there was the urge. It was irresistible, and I was on my feet with a Christmas message that spoke of suffering and spite. I was frightened by what I had done.

No Friend, nor even an experienced attender at Friends meetings of any kind should be afraid of this call. One does not need to be a Quaker to have it. Nevertheless, people are often troubled about knowing when to speak. Though there is never ever any absolute certainty about whether one has been called, there are a few simple ways of testing one's call for oneself.

Since one is engaged on an exercise of discernment, it is important to enquire of oneself as to whether what one feels led to say arises naturally out of personal experience. Is it part of a pattern? Is it grounded in life? Is it a second-hand reflection, or does it come from deep inside? Normally it tests one's faith, for one will have to decide whether the message is about God or whether it comes from God. If the former, one may not give it.

Then there is the meeting. Do the words fit this gathering? Is it part of the exercise of Friends that day? If one has been a member of the meeting for a long while, one should consider how it fits in with the long-term concerns and spiritual needs of the group. If one is in the habit of praying for the meeting, or holding Friends in the light, could this be an opportunity for saying something that needs to be said? There may be bereavements or separations, births or anniversaries, quarrels and reconciliations. They may need to be marked in indirect ways that bring nourishment, challenge or comfort.

This is the sort of concern that arises naturally if one has time in one's life for reflection and prayer—a spiritual discipline. We need personal retirement for communion with God and also space to reflect on the needs of our community. It is always possible that we can leave needs like this to be met by spontaneous and unpremeditated ministry that rushes over us all of a sudden, but I doubt it. It is not necessary to prepare ministry to have given thoughtful consideration to what might be said. What counts is to recognise when God is calling upon us to give it.

I once heard a story from an elderly Friend, who, when young, crassly asked Rufus Jones whether he prepared his sermons. The sage replied that he spent much of his time constructing sermons, but had to wait to be told to give them. I can imagine the twinkle in his eye as he said that, for it puts a profound point. Many people believe Quaker ministry should be spontaneous, ejaculatory and unpremeditated. Such is not the case, provided one has the spiritual discipline to be able to distinguish God's prompting from one's own.

So I do not think Friends need to bother over much if they think they have brought the words to the meeting. It is best to trust one's judgment as to whether one is called upon to deliver them. There are much better ways of getting into a tizzy than trying to decide whether what one has to say is spontaneous or not. That is not the point. One should not ask, "Is it spontaneous?" but "Is it called for?"

This is the point eventually reached by everyone who has ever ministered properly in a Quaker meeting. It is a cause of heart-searching and occasional agony when one cannot decide whether it would be right to stand up and speak. But there is no way round the difficulty, no advice one can give, no help to be proffered. It is like being on the 'exit to system' button on a computer, and no Quaker writer has ever been able to explain it. I think the point is that God approaches each one of us in a highly individual way which is very hard to express. What we can say is that faith, trust, and commitment to Friends' doctrine of the continuing inward and unmediated revelation of God are absolutely essential. Beyond that, one simply has to shove doubt on one side and take the consequences.

This is yet another example of the formative influence of the stillness that arises out of silence. If the ways of God in our experience are like this, what we should do is to wait patiently for the angel to disturb the waters. As a minister, I do what I did when I was a beginner in the art of silence. I structure things, go over the words and try to be sure I have them all safely marshalled. But that is a phase I am leaving behind. I am now being given the gift others have received right at the start. I am beginning to find I can go by feel and can wait for the words to come when I am on my feet.

I find that if I do all these things in an attempt to deny the call, to prevent myself speaking, there are many occasions in which the feeling passes. But there are other times when I feel almost forced to my feet. I find the urge goes away but comes back again more strongly. When it has done this once or twice, I give way to a sort of fatalism. God must be allowed to take over. If it is right, I find myself speaking. If it is not, I remain in my seat. Whichever happens, I know the deep feeling of faithfulness the great Quakers of the past called a baptism. In words or silence, I know I have been touched by God.

The
Call
to
Minister

The first ministry I ever gave in a meeting for worship is still clear in my memory. It was shortly before Christmas, more than ten years after I was admitted into membership of the Society of Friends. I was reflecting on carols, and the thought struck me that the medieval ones had an edge of warmth, innocence and harshness that was absent from many of those from later centuries. They seemed somehow closer to the reality the season is supposed to celebrate.

Then I came to reflect on the practice of many families in hanging a holly wreath on their front door. I have never been at ease with the easy optimism and conviviality of Christmas, so I offered these reflections to the meeting and enquired how many people with holly wreaths on their doors recognised that it was also a crown of thorns.

I got up because I wanted to and had to. The time had come for me to 'appear in the ministry', to use yet another of those expressions from the Quaker phrase book. I did not know it at the time, but all the turmoil and heart-searching I had experienced before getting to my feet was something ministering Friends have known from the beginning.

It is possibly not coincidental that my first ministry was given at Christmas, which in England is usually drab, damp and grey. The weather is a perfect setting for a festival of light, particularly at dusk on the Eve of the Nativity. At that time, I always have the sensation that the world is slowing down, becoming still, waiting with a divine resignation for the singing of the angels and the wheeling stars to stop. One of my private symbols for that peace is the pigeons perching calmly in the trees. At midwinter there are no leaves, and you can see them there.

I love meeting for worship in winter for similar reasons. Though, as a Friend, I am traditionally not supposed to look to outward symbolism for religious truth, the peacefulness of the Christmas season is irresistible. More than at any other time I feel a oneness between my worship and the one to whom it is offered. I am sure those of other churches feel similarly. I can only explain that this is how I come close to the heart of the unprogrammed meeting for worship in the Quaker tradition.

I have also learned that the spoken ministry can be given to the unsuspected need of someone present in the meeting. On another occasion I found myself ministering about the atmosphere in the burial ground outside our meeting house. I said I hoped to be buried there and that its calm and dignity as a place presaged what I hoped the experience of leaving this life would be like. I was well aware of the number of elderly Friends in the meeting, and I was afraid of what I had to say. There was a tinge of impertinence about my words, a lack of consideration perhaps, a sense deep in me that I was treading on holy ground. There is always the ultimate fear I cannot escape from, that uncalled-for ministry is blasphemy.

When the meeting closed, a Friend came up to me, and we fell into a lengthy conversation about what I had said. Soon thereafter, he rang me up out of the blue and told me to come to his house and take instructions for his will. He was insistent. The following week would not do. I was to come immediately. When I went, I was shaken by the deterioration in his physical condition. I produced a will for him in double quick time, and it is as well that I did, for he died within the week.

On that one occasion, at least, I have no doubt that God was calling me directly and personally. I was able to minister to a Friend in great need, and I hope my spiritual comforts were as acceptable as my professional services. I have certainly continued to help my friend's widow where I can. What I said, certainly unpremeditated and unpredictable when I entered the meeting, led to important consequences. Not least of them was my Friend's ministry to me. If I live to be a hundred I shall never encounter anyone who approached the end with such clear-sighted courage, faith, and concern for those who would be left behind.

When I gave this ministry, I was afraid, because I had in mind that many of my hearers would be elderly. But my Friend was in the prime of life, and I could have had no notion of the outcome of my faithfulness. But such it was. I was called to service in a chain of events that went well beyond me, and at that time I had no inkling of its existence. I think that this must be another of the reasons why the point at which we feel the call to minister is awesome. It is desirable and frightening at the same time. It is the nearest I come to understanding the meaning of the word 'holy'.

It is almost impossible to describe the feeling. It is like the welling up of a spiritual wave within or a breaking forth of some invisible glory in the soul. There is a sense of an almost tangible power or strength. One is taught, rightly, to resist the urge to rise and speak when it first comes and to struggle till it becomes irresistible. So it does, as if one has wrestled with an angel.

I think this explains the use of the word 'ministry' to characterise these (usually) short speeches in an unprogrammed meeting. The word is in use because Friends understand them to be expressions of divine truth granted to the person ministering as an act of grace. They are considered to be one of the gifts of the Spirit of which the New Testament speaks.

Friends believe that this call to minister can come to any member of the meeting. It springs in the soul of anyone who has centred down or entered this experience St. Teresa called 'recollection'. There are not two kinds of experience, that of the ministering Friend, and the others. Nevertheless, Friends have always recognised that some of their number receive a special vocation to the ministry. It can come to any member of the meeting, and the tradition reveals a very large number of instances in which Friends have undertaken a particular discipline of prayer and self-examination because they feel that God is beginning to call on them to minister regularly, and personal preparation is the only way to respond.

When we talk about the 'gift' of ministry, we must be careful, for the word can be taken in a number of ways. People are said to have a gift if they enjoy a certain skill or talent, but also, someone has a gift if they have received a present from somebody else.

Among Friends, the call to minister is understood as a divine gift in the latter sense. One can prepare oneself to receive it by striving to become worthy of it, but one cannot fit oneself for it by study or meditation alone. These things can be a help, but on any given occasion words may be given or withheld, and none of one's own reflections can make up for their absence.

So words are a part of the Quaker tradition. If the ministering Friend has been faithful, the words will have come at a cost. If the Friend has not been, the words will not have been spoken 'in the life' as Friends say. One of the skills in listening to ministry is to tell one from the other. This difficulty is also felt by ministers. Part of their struggle, as they strive to find words for the messages that rise in their minds and imaginations, is to distinguish the true divine leading from the purely human one.

I can only know for certain afterwards, when I have physical symptoms that can only be described as quaking. If my words have been in the life, I am in no doubt. I feel dry and weak, as if something has gone out of me. I find the after-meeting politenesses unbearable and have to go away somewhere by myself. This is an odd reaction, because my ministry often does not seem to merit that sort of feeling of responsibility. But it comes, and a lot of Friends will admit to feeling the same.

It must never be presumed that because the call has come once, it will come again. Equally, if it has never come, one must never think it never will. Strictly speaking, all one is called upon to do is to be ready *if* called, and in this, once more, the distinction between the minister and the ordinary worshipper disappears, for in the silence there is no organisational need for a leader, and leading is left to God to choose whom he will.

It has to be said, however, that there are meetings in which there is little sense of divine leading in the spoken ministry, but a lot of reliance of what Friends used to call 'the creature'. These flights of imaginative fancy, intellectual preoccupations and emotional difficulties provide much information about the ministers but not a great deal about God. They are the exception, however. Most meetings are held in deep reliance upon God, and those who minister in these meetings do so out of a sense of responsibility and calling.

The stillness and the speaking are the two poles of a meeting in the unprogrammed Quaker tradition. Some people come to Friends and are attracted immediately by the stillness. Others find that the ministry, quite apart from anything specific that is said, expresses what they feel should be the intimate connection between religion and life. In addition, many find in the directness and spontaneity of the ministry, a spiritual authority they have missed elsewhere.

The great English Friend, Caroline Stephen, who came from an intellectual Cambridge family, wrote of her first meeting:

> ...before the meeting was over, a sentence or two were uttered in great simplicity by an old and apparently untaught man, rising in his place amongst the rest of us. I did not pay much attention to the words he spoke, and I have no recollection of their purport. My whole soul was filled with the unutterable peace of the undisturbed opportunity for communion with God, with the sense that at last I had found a place where I might, without the faintest suspicion of insincerity, join with others in simply seeking His presence. (*Christian Faith and Practice in the Experience of The Religious Society of Friends*, London, #80.)

In a well-ordered meeting the ministry and the silence work together. When Friends individually have centred down, the meeting begins to gather, and often someone will rise and speak at this point. After further quiet, another will rise. Again, if the meeting is rightly ordered, what is then said will take the first message further, and after subsequent contributions, a pattern or a theme emerges.

What happens is that the particular exploration of truth which the ministry is making proceeds one step at a time. Waiting for leading is a Quaker principle of great importance. One does not rush ahead quickly. A sort of dialectic is in process, with different and possibly inconsistent things being said. Then there is a search for a resolution of these things which does justice to them all, and in the midst of private prayer and meditation, the meeting is expected to take part in the process.

This process is called the 'exercise' of the meeting, and the word is another piece of Quakerly jargon which illustrates the unwritten lore surrounding silent worship and the fact that practise in it over a period must be guided, for it can easily be changed into something else. The sense of exercise is somewhat weak these days, possibly because the time set aside for worship is usually the arbitrary hour, and the meeting ends at a time of purely human convenience.

Nevertheless, where a meeting is truly exercised, there is a deep feeling of guidance among those assembled. Towards the end, the spoken word may lapse, as Friends feel united by something stronger than themselves. In the past, such words as 'gathered' or 'covered' were used to describe feelings that are probably not accurately called blissful, but certainly meet the description, 'the peace that passes understanding'.

When early Quaker writers spoke about silent meetings, it was this unity that goes beyond words or the need to give expression to it to which they referred, and every unprogrammed meeting knows this in its own experience. But in modern circumstances it is sometimes difficult to sustain where the basis of a Friends meeting is essentially intellectual or psychological, rather than being grounded in a commonly held faith in a God whose ways are known, understood and loved.

One of the best ways of telling whether a meeting has been gathered is a reluctance to end it. Friends often say that a meeting was not long enough, but what to do about this is difficult. In theory the meeting sits until Friends discern that God is ready to release them, but in modern times this normally means a conventional hour. In practise there are many ways of ending. One meeting house I know is opposite a Salvation Army citadel. When the band across the street strikes up "Onward Christian Soldiers," the Quakers know it is time to go. Someday, someone will continue sitting there, and the process of renewal in London Yearly Meeting will begin.

In passing we should note an interesting sidelight on the process of a meeting becoming exercised. From time to time one hears a minister put into words what one had been thinking oneself. This is not telepathy, though one feels eerie when it happens. Actually it is yet another way of knowing that the meeting is seriously exercised, and it indicates a coming into unity.

Observers of an unprogrammed meeting over an extended period come to recognise that in practise the burden of spoken ministry is carried by relatively few Friends, although there is usually a wider circle of occasional ministers. Each Friend who ministers has his or her own characteristic approach, style, themes and methods. Some initiate the ministry. Some are talented at drawing together the threads of an apparently chaotic or diverse meeting. Some are spiritual in their bias, some political. There are all sorts, and a lucky meeting has the widest possible variety.

In some parts of the Quaker world. Friends who have been given the gift of ministry are 'recorded', that is to say, an entry is made in a minute book somewhere to the effect that the community recognises their call. But the call is still regarded as having come from God, and the record is simply recognition of the fact. It is not an ordination because it confers no special status, and while Friends recognise that some people have a gift, they also understand that each exercise of that gift is a fresh call.

The practise of recording is part of the heritage of Quakerism. In parts of the unprogrammed tradition it is in eclipse, because Friends feel that it discourages those who are not recorded to accept their responsibility to minister. It is also felt to be an invidious or elitist idea. Elsewhere, however, many yearly meetings of the programmed tradition have taken to recording a much wider variety of gifts than just the call to speak, so the institution is being developed creatively in new ways.

In former times, Friends recognised as having the gift came under the care of elders, whose prime duty was to encourage ministry. Theirs was a special vocation to watch over the meeting, and they formed a cadre of souls, deeply experienced in the ways of God, who upheld the gathering meeting in prayer and sustained it by their devotion. Thus, neither the spoken words of the ministers, nor the devotions of individual Friends took place in isolation.

Underneath the silence was the still centre of prayer and concern provided by the body of elders. In many ways, what they did, and still do in many meetings in the unprogrammed tradition, provides the spiritual co-ordination which gives a unity which would otherwise be lacking or coincidental.

Those who were recorded met regularly with elders for worship and mutual advice and support. They deepened their sense of vocation, guided one another through difficult periods and built up the meeting's sense of corporate identity. To see the meeting for worship as the only important feature of spiritual formation in the Society of Friends is a mistake. Traditionally its health has been in a large measure dependent on the way of life which supported it, which was codified in that pattern of life laid before Friends in what is to this day known as 'the Discipline'.

This co-ordination of the life of the meeting is rare nowadays, and unless those who minister in an unprogrammed meeting accept the informal discipline of listening to one another, they can sound repetitive and unco-ordinated. Variety is a great asset to a meeting, but it needs to be controlled and harmonised, and those who minister need a sense of growing together. The tradition provides the means of doing this, but it is a source of considerable difficulty in the unprogrammed tradition today.

It is important that these links are not forgotten, for there is a pastoral dimension to the spoken ministry, after all. To concentrate on its origin in God can be to neglect its destination in the hearts of those in meeting to whom it comes. Ministering Friends are also representatives of their community and need great sensitivity to it. Ideally their own spiritual struggles should reflect, as well as minister to, those to whose service they are called, and it is these whom the elders primarily represent.

The ultimate purpose of worship is to conform us to the image of God, and in this process the minister and the meeting are at one. This is something which takes place over time and is in the form of a dialogue in which we search for divine guidance, seek a revelation of truth, and listen for the prophetic utterance. In the experience of the unprogrammed tradition, this path leads us deep into our own soul, and also involves us deeply in the social and political life around us. There is no part of our lives which can remain untouched.

If the ministry in meetings does not speak to these things, it will be of little value. Religion and life are of one stuff. Meetings for worship are not like isolated islands of holiness which we visit weekly in our rough voyage through oceans of godlessness. The ministry should speak to us of the passing of years, the stages of life, the continuous concern we have with the state of the world, and the revelation of God in these things. It may not be prepared week by week, but it should have continuous concerns and an overarching vision.

Harmony in a religious body comes through a common identity, a telling of the common story, a repetition of the common values, a portrayal of the people the group believes itself to be. Spiritual harmony goes beyond this to a deeper level of value and experience, and if membership of the group is not to consist simply of an assertion of one's right to be different, the seeds of unity must be planted deep. It is the unusual person who is mature enough not to need help in this. It is the spoken ministry which should provide a sense of that into which by God's grace one can grow.

But if Quakers are human, they will be as fractious, disobedient and opinionated as other people. Unity is hard work, and simply to sit in silence ignoring what ministers say without coming to terms with it is an easy thing to do. But it misses one of the essentials. Though we may be perfectible, and though we may be redeemed from the contaminations of the world, we are involved in a struggle with ourselves, and the assumption of spiritual self-sufficiency is likely to be wrong.

Hence the need for challenge in the spoken ministry, both to question the easy assumptions we all make for the sake of comfort and also constantly to prove the dedication of the community to the ideals it has adopted. This element of challenge is particularly important for Friends, who knowingly and willingly adopt the most testing ethical standards. It is no coincidence that Amos 6:1 was the favourite text of many of the itinerant ministers of the past—"Woe to them that are at ease in Zion."

The spoken word is therefore indispensable. It has an honourable history among Friends and an important place in their worship. We shall perhaps understand its significance better if we see Quaker worship as based upon stillness, and the silence and the ministry as dual expressions of that stillness. It is the wellspring from which they both flow.

Making
Decisions

Some time back I attended a large Quaker gathering in the western United States in the company of a very astute journalist who had come to the Society, like me, from another church. The reactions we each had to the regular taking up of collections, the Sunday best clothes and the gospel hymns got me thinking about the other side of Quakerism. My Friend had been used to the liturgical tradition which, I have suggested, is the chief source of silent worship within Christianity. He had forsaken the ritual but retained the silence. I think he found it hard to make out how these rowdy goings-on could possibly be connected with what he knew as Quakerism.

Oddly enough, I had no such troubles, because the circumstances of my early life had equipped me, almost instinctively, to deal with existence of Quakers and Quaker meetings which get along perfectly well without much silent worship. In the unprogrammed tradition, there is often a tacit assumption that Quakerism is defined by silence, and other things are secondary to that. So you are liable to some kind of culture-shock when you go among programmed Friends, unless you can begin to see that Quakerism in the round is rather more than what you see in your own mirror.

I am at home in programmed meetings because of the advantage of my childhood. Like so many other children in

England at the outbreak of the Second World War, I became an 'evacuee', someone sent away from the city as a protection against the bombing. I went to live with my grandparents in a little cottage on the edge of Dartmoor in the far west of England. My father was a soldier, my mother a cook on an air base, my grandfather a retired policeman turned farm labourer, and my Gran kept the home. Till my mother returned to produce my sister, it was little short of paradise.

I attended the Baptist church in the small town nearby. The river ran outside, the Sunday School hall was in the basement, and we used to scramble up winding wooden staircases to get to the vestry and the choir entrances which were on either side of the church. Until I was in my teens and began to attend the Episcopalian church to which my scout group was attached, I had never seen an altar, a crucifix, a clergyman in vestments, or a stained-glass window from the inside.

Not until much later on—when I began to take my Quakerism seriously, in fact—did I fully comprehend why this was. The little country church had an impressive pedigree. The English Baptists were originally Puritans—part of that great seventeenth-century movement which, whatever its faults, stood for integrity in religion, democracy in politics, and government of the church by the people who made it up. I knew nothing of all that as a small boy. But I knew that this little church was for our kind of people. You don't need to be taught things like that. If I had come first to the programmed tradition in Quakerism via the unprogrammed variety, if I had been a humanist or secularist of some sort, or a Catholic, an Orthodox or an Episcopalian, used to liturgical worship, I would have had no particular reason to attach any importance to the Puritan heritage of Quakerism. I have heard Friends of the unprogrammed tradition say, "Oh, I went to a programmed meeting once. It didn't have much to do with Quakerism." Such words are naive. The revelation of God that comes to you in a particular church tradition is given over time. You cannot have it in an hour. Once.

Though I have probably given the impression that I see silent worship after the manner of Friends as part of its heritage from the Catholic part of western Christendom, the balance needs to be corrected. My own religious journey took me from the nonconformist chapels of my childhood to the Episcopal Church of England (for a while) and thence to the silence of unprogrammed Quaker meetings. The reason that I feel at home in programmed Quaker meetings is that there I come back to my roots—the stiff-necked but generous Protestantism of the English dissenters, the self-employed craftsmen and small traders who have produced most of the good things in English history. George Fox came from that class. So did my father. So do I.

I sat at that big Quaker conference hugging these thoughts to myself. I already knew them as a matter of history, but I was now beginning to glimpse their continuing importance as one of the sources of the vitality of the Society of Friends. When I first joined it in England I knew nothing of all this. But I have come to realise that important relationships have all sorts of consequences one has not anticipated. When I got married, I acquired a new family as well as a spouse, and the more I found out about her family, the better I understood my wife. What do they know of silence who only silence know?

It ought to be clear by now that silent worship involves a great deal more than the absence of words. It is the main form of growth and schooling for the unprogrammed tradition and the greatest symbolic expression of the Quaker faith for programmed meetings. It sometimes looks like a way of worship with a loose religious organisation attached, but that is far from the truth. The form of worship enshrines Friends understanding of the church—disciples come together to listen and to hear.

This is the point of unity between those Friends who have worship services and those who meet in silence. Behind the form of worship that is visible of a Sunday in a programmed meeting or a Friends Church, there stands a vision of the Christian community which has no place for hierarchy, even that of the ordained minister called by the congregation. Despite appearances to the contrary, the Quaker pastor is an ordinary Friend released for service and not a person set aside to exercise special gifts. Thus, in a programmed meeting the decision making process is exactly like its counterpart in the unprogrammed tradition.

For a meeting is more than simply a worshipping community. It is a group of people living in the world and facing the challenge of witnessing to it. Worship can lead far beyond what one does on Sunday. Meeting for worship can be more than just an occasion on which one's private religious needs are satisfied. Silent devotion should lead to an awareness that the meeting is less and less a place we choose ourselves, and more and more a place to which, out of love, God has called us. To understand this is to sense the meaning of those lovely phrases about the community of faith being the body of Christ.

Early Friends knew, practised and cherished this unity of spirit. They called it 'gospel order', for they felt the presence of the Lord among them, guiding and leading, so strongly that they dispensed with any human assistant or intermediary. But they were not the individualists of their detractors' imaginations. They had a close feeling of being together, irrevocably, for the nature of the light was to call people into fellowship.

The silence in which Friends assemble to worship, or which they uphold at the centre of their programmed devotions, is a sign of this community, and amid all the controversies and differences with which their history is littered, they know it. We have defined convincement and conversion in Quaker terms as the transcendence of self and a coming to wait upon the leadings of God in all things. The meeting for business cannot be understood in isolation, it is part of a spiritual discipline.

The focus of worship is therefore upon the community coming before God in response to the divine initiative. Waiting in silence is a sign of obedience, openness, willingness to receive guidance. It is an acknowledgment of our own fallibility. Formerly it was seen as the primary place for discerning how faith could be applied to new circumstances under divine guidance and the testing of individual leadings against the common understanding of scripture and the collective spiritual experience.

This spiritual experience needed no great ceremony. Nor were the historic Quaker synods noted for the new apprehensions of truth which they were granted. Rather, for Friends, the really big issues in the life of faith are made up of an infinite number of small ones. Week by week, month by month, year by year, meeting by meeting, the clear warming light leads deeper and deeper into the mystery of God.

The epitome of this Quaker understanding of the church is found in programmed and unprogrammed meetings alike. Robert Barclay, writer of the first systematic essay on this matter, took the church in the Acts of the Apostles as his conscious model. He poined out that immediately after Pentecost the church organized care for the poor—by implication, the satis-faction of the bodily needs of the community of the faithful.

Not quite playfully, (if we have the courage to follow Barclay), we could suggest that the meeting for church affairs, the business meeting, is the more important assembly of the Society of Friends and not its public meetings for worship. That would seem to be in right ordering, but it somehow goes against the grain. How on earth could we defend such an extraordinary assertion?

A good beginning would be to look with fresh eyes at the practise of not voting in business meetings. So deeply is the practise of voting entrenched in democratic societies that newcomers to Friends meetings sometimes find it difficult to attune to. What makes matters worse is that there are Friends perfectly accustomed to electioneering and vote-getting as part of their public lives, who would never dream of doing such things among their own kind.

Instead, they are familiar with the practise of an ordinary member of the meeting, called the clerk, sitting at a table, listening, occasionally writing, and finally producing a short note called a 'minute' which appears to record what the assembled Friends have decided to do. The business meeting is a meeting for worship, and it takes place on the basis of silence just like any other meeting.

Thus, exactly the same discipline of waiting in stillness is required. One is expected to attend in order to discern God's will for the assembly, not to argue for one's own point of view. Thus, a willingness to be persuaded is essential. There are often pauses between contributions as there are between pieces of ministry, and without the discipline of silent waiting, it would be impossible for the process to carry the theological weight Friends claim for it. What is of great significance is the spirit in which it is held and the religious assumptions made about what is going on.

These do not make a great deal of sense when applied to decisions like what colour to paint the front door of the meeting house. But in accordance with the principle that if you are faithful in little, you will be faithful in much, Friends find that when they have great differences of principle about important matters, it is their peculiar institutionalised form of practising their faith which brings them through.

Crucial to the process is the clerk, who sits 'at the table' and is the servant of the meeting. The function of the clerk is to write out the minute, and this is done on the basis of what is said. Some clerks record much of the discussion, others are terse. Some are renowned for their capacity to lead meetings in difficulty, others for their style of recording. Some are brisk, some let their meetings ramble. No two are alike.

The role of the clerk is defined by the minute, and it is at this point that much of the traditional practise of Quakerism has been misunderstood. There are Friends who think that a meeting is an exercise in pure democracy. Everybody should have a say and state what they feel. They should try to be as conciliatory as they can, so that at the end of the discussion the clerk can sum up what has been said in a nice minute that contains the highest common factor of agreement, and Friends can then get on to the next piece of business.

The word 'consensus' is often used in this connection, and one is embarrassed to have to claim that the Quaker business meeting is not an exercise in consensus decision-making. Doing things by agreement and compromise is a sign of considerable maturity in a person or an organisation. If there were more consensus in the world, it would be a far more peaceful place. It is not the value of consensus that is at issue, but whether that is what a Quaker business meeting should be seeking.

The rub comes in seeing the meeting as a democratic assembly. Consider what is being done for a moment. If the clerk is looking for the general sense of the meeting, he or she will be trying to make a minute that will reflect what is said. Therefore, the minute will be the servant of the meeting. But, on the other hand, if the assembled Friends are concerned not to obtain a decision in their own wisdom, but intend instead to seek the guidance of God, the meeting will be the servant of the minute.

This looks like a verbal quibble, but in fact it goes to the root of the understandings and misunderstandings of Quaker business that one even finds among Friends nowadays. This is Barclay's point. Pastoral care is priority of the community. It is not something of a lower grade of religious importance. So meetings for business are meetings for worship and should be held accordingly.

The traditional presuppositions of the Quaker business meeting are not really sustainable on any other basis. Clearly, if people do not believe there is a God, or that God's will is ascertainable, this approach will be impossible. But Friends have always asserted that God's will *is* discoverable in this way. One of the ways of discerning it is through the guidance given to other members of the meeting. Hence they attend meetings for business in a frame of mind which expects that the meeting will issue in unity, that guidance can come from anyone there, and, therefore, the participation of everybody is important.

This demands considerable spiritual maturity, for what is required is a willingness to listen to what others have to say rather than to persuade them that one's own point of view represents what is right and proper. It also requires restraint. The reiteration of one point by several Friends each in their own way lends no weight to the point. What the meeting must learn to discern is its rightness, not how many people support it.

This is why there are no votes and why a minority in a meeting can always frustrate the will of the majority. Friends are willing to sacrifice the despatch of business efficiently to the principle that the minority may be in the right, so that one of the best guides to the divine will is to wait patiently until the meeting is enabled to go forward in unity.

Moreover, in matters of great importance, it is often found that there is no way for a consensus view to be arrived at, even if it were sound in principle to attempt one. Where Friends are willing to adjust their views in matters of controversy, it is because they have loyalty to a higher truth, not because they wish to compromise for the sake of avoiding conflict. It would be easy to see these few brief remarks about how Friends do their business as quite a simple process of compromise dressed up in religious language and not really amounting to very much. People who think that can be forgiven, but the proof comes in the practise.

There are many, many Friends, not given to self-deception, who will vouch for these things from their own experience. When conflict comes, as it does, and the temptation to compromise— to seek consensus—is resisted, the sense of divine guidance is unmistakably registered. New possibilities for a way forward which nobody has thought of emerge out of discussion. Postponement and delay settle minds and assist the process of coming to a united mind. Above all, those who take opposing views come to find that the discipline of waiting has mysteriously united them.

Beautiful as the unprogrammed meeting for worship is, it is the minority practise among Friends in the world. It can only be definitive of Quakerism by excluding the majority. Not so the business method, which is practised in pastoral and unpro- grammed meetings alike, and which, properly practised, has all the features of a 'silent' meeting. It is in doing business that the characteristic process of spiritual discernment in the manner of Friends is truly found, and silent worship is important to those of us who practise it for that reason and not the reverse. And it is the basis of our bond with our brothers and sisters of the programmed tradition.

Thus, Robert Barclay has pointed Friends to the soil out of which the spiritual life of their community springs. Business meetings have a premier place in schooling us in listening to God. They are a sign and an example to the world of how we could all live in a reconciling spirit. They are the first place to which the concerns laid upon individuals are brought. They train us to hear the kernel of truth in the utterances of others as we learn to look through complications and distractions with a simple eye. They are the basis of our ministry and our common life and are where the source of our unity is to be found.

Beyond the Quaker Meeting

Celebration
and
Sacrifice

Much of what is valuable in our lives happens in community. We are born of the union of two people. We grow up as members of a family. We have a neighbourhood, a nation, a history and a future. If our conception of religion fails to acknowledge the social dimension of life, we shall not do it justice. Important though our private relationship with God may be, we are called into a kingdom, into fellowship, into dependence upon other people. The central act of Christian worship is an affirmation of these things.

The first time I ever took Holy Communion was by mistake. I had been invited to take the service at a Congregational church near where I was living, and I followed my usual practise of worshipping with the congregation for a week or two beforehand so I did not come cold to a group of people I had not got to know. On this occasion it was the second of my visits, and the whole thing was a disaster from start to finish.

The board registered six hymns. I thought that odd because the week before there had been only four. There was a bigger congregation too, and I was crammed into a box pew with at least half a dozen people between me and the aisle. When the minister came in, he announced that as it was communion Sunday, there would be the usual collection for Oxfam, and everybody had to give lots of money. Unhappily, I had come out in a hurry with *no money at all,* and I had the undignified necessity of explaining myself to the deacon as being forgetful rather than ungenerous. He was very kind about it, but I felt a fool.

Moreover I then had a terrible crisis of conscience. I had never ever participated in the supper of the Lord before. Perhaps because it is, and was, so important to me, I was strongly disinclined. Not only did it feel unfaithful to all my principles as a Friend, but I just did not feel worthy. I never do. It is never just a memorial for me. I am always present in Jerusalem. However, with deep prayer and heart-searching, coupled with the fear of being standoffish and the impossibility of escape, I decided to take part.

But God, being a humorist, did not let me off lightly. In one of the churches of another tradition, I might have waited piously while others went up to the front to receive the elements. Here they were brought to me. First, I was offered a tray on which there was a little ball of bread. I took it and did not know what to do with it. Eat or wait? No gambler ever had such an agonising decision. I waited, and that was right. When I received my thimbleful of wine, I was prepared.

It may be hard for non-Friends to realise quite the turmoil I was in. There is nothing like being the odd one out to shake one's self-confidence. Quaker principles about outward observance are easily maintained among other Friends. In the wider Christian community, they are sometimes questioned. What seems obvious on the meeting house bench can be altogether more problematic when one is away from it.

This experience raised in an acute form the question of my own identity as a worshipper. It made me think about myself and what I was doing and also about the community in which I did it. One of the most seductive features of worship in silence is that the individual can become so absorbed in personal concerns that the sense of belonging to a community and taking part in its collective worship can be seriously weakened.

I reflected on these things during the service and realised that I was at a point where two lines of history intersected. This account of my life as a Quaker describes the personal part, the experience of an ordinary person and the influences at work in his life to make him what he is. But then there is the collective part. I have to recognise that I have willingly joined myself to a larger whole and part of me must be defined by it. While I must at all costs preserve my honesty and integrity, I also have to admit that I am limited in knowledge and experience and, there is a collective authority I must pay attention to. Being a Quaker does not just mean being myself. I have to go beyond to what I can be, and the public part of Quakerism is my means for doing that.

The other line of history is that of the Society of Friends, and my attitude to the communion service was coloured by its own doctrine on the matter. I certainly understood it, but the question was being subtly put to me as to whether I took it seriously. I concluded that I did, but not in its strict form. I was able to take part in the supper of the Lord in good conscience because I was willing to look at it in a certain way.

My starting point was not the objections to sacramental observance Quakers usually make, but a sense of the passing of time and the tendency for all human associations to throw up what is for me a great richness of diversity. I grow increasingly convinced that the longer the view we take of our own identity, the closer we see ourselves to other people. If we can see how our own religious group is the product of a tension between its need to be its own individual self and its need to belong to wider family groups, we shall be a lot more tolerant of others and easy-going on ourselves. I do not like zealots and purists, of the Quaker or any other variety.

The historical process seems to me to issue in different forms of self-awareness. We give expression to our values through the groups we belong to and identify with. The story of God's saving action in Christ is a long and complicated one, so it does not surprise me that within that overall framework, different groups of Christians find certain specific events or emphases more important than others. These things lend character to them and give them their distinctiveness.

As I look at patterns of devotion and worship I tend to draw a broad distinction between Last Supper and Pentecost churches. The former prepare for and re-enact the self-sacrifice of Christ in meticulous detail. The latter look for the power and guidance of his spirit. But it is a matter of emphasis rather than principle. What is at issue is the relative value a religious group places on different parts of its own story and therefore what it considers more significant. Plainly there are churches for whom the Eucharist is a supreme expression of discipleship, and they put a high value on tradition, hierarchy, ceremony and outward symbolism. Equally plainly there are the churches who have a minimum of these things and stress the equality of believers, the importance of personal conviction and discipleship based on the power of the Holy Spirit. Spontaneity is rated higher than right order.

It is clear where the Quakers stand. Silent worship is based on pentecostal expectation and has a biblical and theological rationale which will support a continuing tradition. Failing this, worship in silence is possible, but it will be something quite different from what this tradition has normally understood meeting for worship to involve. It is the collective aspect that is at issue—whether silence alone is a sufficient basis for a worshipping community.

Clearly, it is not. Religious communities are bound together by far more things than their manner of worship. If I remove my Quaker-tinted spectacles,I see a community within the Christian Church which has developed its own distinctive practises over a wide range of matters. In dress, speech, ethical codes, the deliberate avoidance of special festivals, folklore, history, foundation myth, initiation processes, organisational principles, beliefs, prayer, and spirituality, as well as methods of worship, the Religious Society of Friends is different in form but similar in substance to many other religious groups. It is not as unique as it thinks.

It is possible to conclude that defining Quakerism in terms of its worship is putting the cart before the horse or, perhaps, picking out only one of its features as its defining characteristic to the exclusion of other equally important things. The contrary view will see the insight of a particular group of Christians into the nature of their faith as the wellspring of their distinctive worship. The public aspect is primarily remembrance, the private aspect, experience. The ideal is harmony between the two.

Perhaps the most important function of public worship is to tell the story of the group, how it began, what it has been through and how God has dealt with it. In most churches the practise of baptising and observing the Lord's Supper is a living reminder of the life of Jesus and provides a direct, two thousand-year-old link with his first disciples. Observing the seasons of the year, like Lent and saints' days has the same effect. This is one of the reasons for reading the Bible publicly, and the same message is repeated over and over again in hymns.

In a silent Friends meeting there is no programme of public observance like this, and in recent decades this has resulted in a marked decline in spoken ministry dealing with the major themes of the Christian life. That is not to say that such ministry has disappeared, but generally it is weaker than it was. But this has led to an interesting development.

There are certain Quaker figures whose stories express the values and concerns of many contemporary Friends of the unprogrammed tradition. John Woolman, Isaac Penington, James Nayler, Margaret Fell, Rufus Jones and Lucretia Mott are characters from the Quaker past who provide a constant inspiration by what they did and said, and in miniature they are seen to express the essence of Quakerism. Brief extracts from their writings occur in the official handbooks of the various autonomous yearly meetings among Friends, and frequent reference is made to them in spoken ministry.

Hence, despite the lack of outward formality, the silent meeting still functions as a public acknowledgment by the community of the grounds for its being, and though there is formally a complete freedom for the gathered Friends to follow the leadings of the Spirit, it usually utilises a conventional wisdom or record of some sort.

For example, in 1652, George Fox, the founder of the Society of Friends, climbed a mountain called Pendle Hill in Lancashire, England. There he says he saw a vision of "a great people waiting to be gathered." This story is often told as an illustration of the hope and gratitude of Friends that they have been called into that company of people and have thus inherited the mantle of the great Quakers of history.

Another example is the visit made by John Woolman of Mount Holly, New Jersey, to an Indian village in circumstances of great danger towards the end of the French and Indian War in 1763. Talking to him through an interpreter, a chief said, "I like to feel where words come from." Friends love this story as an example of their faith that the inward light is universal, and love can be expected to respond to love.

So behind the silent meeting and the ministry that is given in it, glimpses can be discerned of a very rich particular tradition which is always understated. But it is there, even if many in the unprogrammed tradition do not always appreciate the fact, and the silent worship often produces ministry which invites Friends to make an imaginative entry into the circumstances of the past. This is an exact parallel with the more formal worship service but on a much looser basis.

The silence in the midst of a programmed meeting is often called 'communion after the manner of Friends'. Similarly, many Friends of the unprogrammed tradition will say that in their meetings there is a holy communion without the outward signs. Nevertheless, there are serious traditional objections to putting things like this, as we shall see. Though Friends generally do not observe the Lord's Supper as a memorial at regular intervals, nor give formal acknowledgment to the Christian year, they will insist that communion is an essential part of their worship, as is remembrance of Christ in their midst. That is the reality which inspired, in their own time, the great figures of the Quaker past.

The Lord's Supper, the great central act of Christian worship, operates at many levels and can be explained theologically in a variety of ways. It is certainly the public expression of a divine mystery. To the mystical temperament it is a foretaste of heaven. In its symbolism it stands for the only gift humanity can offer its creator to match the one it has received—life itself. The eucharist is an outward sign of many things: a longing for unity and faithfulness, a common sharing of the bread of life, struggle and penitence, thanksgiving and praise, love and reconciliation, a vision of the restoration of all things into unity with Christ, the acquisition of strength by our taking his fortitude into ourselves. It announces salvation, demands commitment and anchors the Christian faith securely in the world of political reality and historical process.

It is a paradox, like so much in the faith. An earthly event is the vehicle for truths about God. In an upper room, which is recreated in our imagination, a man celebrates a festival with his friends. He points to what will shortly happen to him and makes the memory of a past sacrifice into the portent of a new one, in which the victim will be himself. Whether or not we are at a formal remembrance of this event, whatever worship we offer as Christians is conditioned by it. The nature of this sacrifice is the substance of the Christian's faith.

So when we come to worship in an unprogrammed meeting, no memory of Christ will be without this dimension. Whatever faith we have will be laid at the feet of him who was there. Our exercise of self-knowledge our reflections on our personal relations; our troubles and our needs the reassurance we receive, and the risks we request courage to run are all part of that encounter. We are called to be there too.

This way of looking at worship is based on the faith that it is a relationship to which there is more than one party. This relationship grows out of our way of life, and the purpose of our private devotions and the exercise of the silent meeting is to nourish it and bring it to fruition. As with all worship, it has two sides. There is the offering we bring to God and the blessing we receive in return.

So as worshippers, we might be asked what it is we want when we enter the sanctuary, and what it is we, bring. There is no immediately obvious answer in a silent Quaker meeting, so we have to look within. If we bring a gift to God, we acknowledge his lordship and the need to be released from bondage. If we seek communion, we must come in a body, for we cannot have it alone. If we really come because we seek the presence and knowledge of God, we have to be prepared to yield up the most precious thing we have—life itself.

These are the deep mysteries of Christianity. A sacrifice brings forth a celebration. This is the Mass, the Liturgy, Holy Communion, the supper of the Lord. Quakers do not have it in any recognisable or conventional form, nor is their meeting for worship in any sense the recreation of the Last Supper as the tradition understands it. Nevertheless, at the deepest level, the same process and encounter are there. If we have faith in the real presence of Christ, there can be no other way.

It is in this setting that the individual will find a general expression of particular experience, and through the exercise of the meeting, or through spoken ministry, will be able to contribute to it. Sensation plays no part in the public worship of the unprogrammed tradition. Their story does not allow it. Among the Friends of the programmed tradition, however, one will find the use of words, music and pictorial representations familiar in other churches. There is a small genre of Quaker painting, but it is more familiar and loved in the Friends churches than the meeting houses.

On the other hand, silence encourages a certain kind of reflectiveness in worship. Possibilities for change and development are set out in terms of the inherited code of conduct and habits of thought in the spoken ministry and the assumptions implicit in the social life of the meeting. Central to the old style silent meeting was the preaching of the 'cross', and we have lost a little of the sense of how this central conception related a range of what might otherwise be quite random practises. Historically it is the link between the personal and the collective, the apparent repose of quietness and the intense striving that accompanied the worship that went on in it. As the key element in Quaker spirituality it is what gave clarity, purpose, shape and content to the outwardly formless assembly. Under everything that has been said so far there is the conviction that it remains so today.

The
Power
and the
Light

When I went through the experience I have compared to the traditional Quaker convincement, I learned for the first time that God was working in me as well as through me. I am bold enough to call it convincement because it was a change, a beginning, a landmark all at once. It turned upside down the way I had always looked at religion.

Part of the experience was that I was ready to recognise that I was really quite an ordinary person, while at the same time learning for the very first time how important I was, quite independent of any of the name tags the world put on me. No longer was I a layman, a communicant, a dissenter, a Friend, a footslogger in the church militant, an angel in the church triumphant, somebody who had to fit into some ecclesiastical slot, I was *myself.* I remember with wonder the first time I realised that I could talk authoritatively about the Christian faith on the basis that I had a right to, simply because it was mine. I knew as much about what matters as the Pope.

The experience would not have become a conversion unless it had begun to make changes in my life. I have described the attitudes I began to discern as central to Christian discipleship, but I also discovered a mildly frightening freedom. I came to a quite different estimate of who Jesus was, how he worked, and what sort of relationships with him are possible. My conversion (in the traditional Quaker sense) became a growth in grace and a process of following the will of God as shown in the life of Christ rather than following the example and teaching of Jesus.

My earlier faith was of the example and teaching kind. It was good-hearted and idealistic. I do not wish to denigrate it in any way whatsoever, for it remains the faith of many thousands of Friends in the unprogrammed tradition, and it was the faith of the man, my father, who gave me the gift of a different kind of belief. So I must exercise care in describing how I came to give it up. I must also say that it was with heavy heart that I came to recognise more of my new faith in the Quaker spiritual tradition than the one I had forsaken.

It went without saying in my earlier life that since the world was progressing to better things, religion should change with the world, for it was the source of the ideals of liberty, equality and fellowship which motivated those forces that were striving for change. Underneath my political dreams and my youthful religious seeking there was some such vision of the City of God.

This vision is still with me, but the nature of the ideals it expresses have changed. The danger with progressive faith is that ultimately it has to take the world's standards and conform to them, and it becomes reductionist. It must yield up its own authority in the interest of its ideals. I suppose what happened to me is that I came to see the meaning of this world as an expression of the reality of the next, not the other way round.

In cold print this is quite a neutral matter. But it led me to start saying things and adopting positions that were out of keeping with what many of my friends and relatives and members of the meeting thought. There was occasional shock and hurt and an intellectual counter-attack. I felt as if people were losing faith in me and that I had betrayed them.

As if in self-protection, but in fact in keeping with what was happening to me, I had to begin the long struggle against self-assertiveness. I had to learn to accept the scorn of those for whom the sort of things I now believed were things they considered they had left behind. There was a humiliation I had never known before in many things people said. I began to feel that I was a renegade and was unsound.

The process was therefore a painful one. I was struggling to discern the nature of the spiritual change that was coming over me and to resist anything that might weaken my resolve to see it through. I was learning to confess my sins and to seek grace to overcome them. Later on, when I came to read the great Quaker journals with some insight, I discovered that Friends used to talk about 'The Cross' quite freely, in a way that my contemporaries in the unprogrammed tradition do not. If I had ever heard ministry about that, I should not have been so bitterly lonely at an important time in my life.

The cross and the light are so intimately connected that I doubt whether one can have the one without the other. Certainly in the Quaker tradition it was not possible. If the cross is the name of an experience, light is the name of a power. Unhappily we nowadays associate the light with understanding and the mental side of our lives. The old Quakers knew it by what it did and the relationship they had with it. The light was the basis for their understanding of God.

Roughly, the light was conceived as the means of Christ's intercourse with us, convincing, challenging, guiding and consoling us personally. There was one light, of which there was a measure in each one of us; we did not have our own individual share of it. Thus the light was the principle and source of all the unity we have with one another. As the source of all true doctrine, it showed us how we are to understand the Bible, and without contradicting what that volume says, it gave us new insights by its continuing revelation.

The light turns out to be the key concept in the Quaker reinterpretation of the Christian faith and is often confusing in its implications. The experience of God in the light of Christ enabled Friends, notably George Fox and William Penn, to organise the whole body of Christian doctrine in a new way, reassessing the position and importance of a number of items of belief. Chiefly, their understanding of the light made a radical change in the way the New Covenant was understood, and thence their understanding of the work of Christ.

This understanding led them to their distinctive principles of church order, which involved to a totally free ministry and a rejection of ordination and the sacraments. This created a community of a particular kind, and these congregations developed a radically new method of collective spiritual discernment in their manner of doing business by waiting on the guidance of the light to which they had all individually come.

The outcome of this kind of devotion is found in the

Testimonies. They round off and adorn a whole way of being, a whole manner of coming into relationship with God. There is little here that may not be paralleled in other traditions, but what has traditionally been called Quakerism is the way practise and devotion form an integral whole.

I was a Friend of a number of years' standing before I realised that Quakerism offered not just an acceptable set of values, but a different kind of spiritual life. I became a Quaker as the wholeness of this way of life dawned on me, and I began consciously to rediscover it and repossess it. It was overlain with the ashes of nineteenth-century controversies and twentieth-century uncertainties. Its vocabulary was archaic, its present practitioners very few and mostly in America. But when my father's death put the real questions of life to me and I needed support, I had already heard its echo, and it made sense of what subsequently happened to me.

I have noticed about myself that there are certain levels of religious activity, certain depths which correspond to what I actually do in my faith life. On the surface, we all have notional or habitual beliefs, often largely explained by custom. I like to celebrate Christmas, for example, but the true date of the nativity is something I do not consider important.

One step deeper is my acceptance of the importance of the events in the life of Christ as something we should remember, recount, reflect upon, take into ourselves. I believe these things because they are in the Bible, and they give a framework to my life of worship. But they are at the level of acceptance. They do not really command the loyalty of anything other than my mind. (Though that is not a matter of small importance!)

But of those self-same stories, one stands out. Also, it is the best attested historically: that the man Jesus of Nazareth was crucified in Jerusalem in the time of Pontius Pilate. My response to this story, as the light within me illuminates it, involves more than belief. I do not simply note a fact of history. The church presents me with a challenge to my way of life. It asks for faith, not belief. If I respond to the story, I have moved to another level—from acceptance to commitment.

But there is a deeper level still. The light is not a sign of God, an image, a model, an idea. It is the presence of the divine without intermediary, and independent of all created things. It is the real presence. What I am offered goes even beyond faith. I am called into the presence of truth. Commitment goes far, but at this point abandonment is called for.

If this is perhaps the sequence of the mystical search, it is also the spiritual progression of the classical Quaker experience. From notional or habitual religion we are called by the light to a convincement, which in turn must give rise to a conversion of life. The aim and ideal of faithfulness is that of a perfect obedience, so the doctrine of perfection came to be the crown of Quakerism. As the early Friends used to say, what is the use of being saved in sin? Christ came to save us from it.

The usual responses to a suggestion that we should aim at perfection are surprise, alarm and suspicion, and naturally so. Our own honesty tells us we are not perfect. Our natural modesty wishes to avoid self-righteousness or complacency. History and psychology would seem to deny the possibility on any large scale. We are part of a world we know to be imperfect, and we are involved in moral dilemmas we can often solve only by compromise with our principles.

In one sense that is all true, though I imagine that the earliest Quakers would have had little patience with such considerations. They were quite straightforward. When Jesus says, don't swear, it means just that. If he says, be perfect, it must be possible, and we must put our minds to it. Such was their sense of the power of the light that, while none of them declared personally that they were perfect, they had to insist on it if they were to be consistent in their battle against the doctrine of our inveterate sinfulness which they opposed as unworthy of true followers of Christ.

For early Friends, perfection was the overcoming of sin, that which is contrary to the will of God. Friends were not so unrealistic as not to know that we make mistakes, do wrong things, succumb to temptation, and fail in our self-imposed disciplines. But they did distinguish between acts of sin and the power of sin in a life at a deep level.

Commitment is at the root of faith, and it is interesting in this connexion to see how some of Jesus' words fit together. He always forgave 'sins'. As everybody knows, the gospel knows no inviolable rules. But knowing that our attitudes to money are a good indication of our attitudes to God, he warned people that their hearts would be where their treasure was. Thus, sin consists not in breaking the rules in the acts of this life, but in the hardness of heart which will not love others and thereby cuts off its owner from God.

If therefore, we are to try to be perfect, it is in our hearts that such perfection will be found. Until my conversion began, I could not begin to understand what the doctrine of perfection was getting at. This was because I thought in terms of ethical rules and principles and 'sin' as falling short of an ideal. But I now look for life in the power of God, and I think in terms of growth and fruitfulness.

Hence, the Quaker tradition also contains the helpful and reassuring doctrine of 'measure'. We do not all have the fullness of light. Perhaps that is impossible in this world. But we are all given enough to have something to live up to. It will be challenging and difficult in parts, but it will not present us with things that are too big for us to handle. All that is required from us is faithfulness to live up to measure we are given. When we have done that, we will be given more.

In this, as in so many other things, the Quaker tradition reveals the way it tends to see things as processes, capable of growth and variation, rather than concrete or abstract entities. I do not profess to know whether I can be perfect, but I know that the religious tradition of my adoption, taken seriously, assures me that I can. This is the point of conversion. If I can struggle with my sins and at the same time seek to lose myself in the grace of God, the power the light will give me will enable me to overcome all things.

These changes, wrought in me over some time, taught me to look at people in a new way. When I was speaking in Glasgow once, Friends decided that it would be nice to have a trip to see a famous art collection in the city during the free Saturday afternoon. Some eyebrows were raised when I announced my intention of going to Parkhead to see Glasgow Celtic play football. I was the only one. Football is a working-class sport in Scotland. It is for the uneducated.

I am afraid I was rather naughty. In ministry the following day there was much talk about beauty, artifice, proportion, God's goodness to us and so forth. I resisted the urge to get up and say that Friends were being seduced by some statues and a few old pots. I had stood shoulder to shoulder with some of the riveters, welders, draughtsmen and labourers who had made the finest ships in the world until the shortsightedness of their rulers killed the Clyde. There was strength, compassion, imagination and skill in those men. Also cynicism, indifference, violence and excess. They were all of a piece.

Jesus would have been at Parkhead, not in the Jerusalem Museum. Yes, that was where there was a great people waiting to be gathered. The wheel had come full circle for me. Human beings after my conversion were no longer candidates for Utopia, known best through statistics. I have always loved people, but my love was now changed. The gospel is about freedom now, not a mortgaged future. It is the kingdom we need, not an ideal society. Frighteningly (for a liberal) I began to see the merits of a message of personal salvation.

If I was coming to see people in a new way, I was also coming to see God in a new way too. This was the most difficult lesson. The God I was now in touch with was bigger than I had ever imagined, certainly bigger than the church, and way beyond the cage constructed for him out of theological textbooks and ecclesiastical architecture. At the same time, God was surprising—always there before me, waiting for me to catch up, but close and intimate too. I learned that the grander the human image we make up, the harder God is to find. I found that my constant companion never asked me for more than I could give. God was a bit like me, in fact, and unkindness, the root of all evil made God angrier than anything else. God was always there, and as time went by, I began to get uncanny glimpses of the carpenter of Nazareth.

The last noteworthy thing I learned was to stop making plans. It was really this which turned me into a Christian and a Quaker of the traditional temperament. It marked my arrival at the last stage in my little scheme of spiritual depth. The first time you ever dive off the top board there is a split second you will always remember when there is no going back. You are a millimetre from regaining your foothold on the board, but it could be as far away as the moon. When you have nothing you are free. And that is where real power lies. That is liberation and salvation. That is where I found God.

Quaker
Sacramentalism

It could be that the soul has gone out of our culture. Long ago, Nietzsche wrote that God is dead. If he was right, the twentieth century has experienced the death of the humanity made in that defunct image. So an examination of how we got into this state is an urgent necessity. To have one's confessional feelings ruffled, one's Quakerly sensibilities disarranged, one's conventional attitudes jolted in the process is a quite trivial matter. There are more important things at stake in the world than correct Quakerism.

If Friends are to enter this debate constructively, they are going to have to know what they are talking about. Havering about the precise shade of meaning one gives to one's conception of God is precisely the act of murder Nietzsche's lunatic was raving about. When the world needs a message, the Quakerism that can only ask it questions is not going to get very far. Neither is the Quakerism which offers little more than a version of mainstream protestantism with historical frills.

The peace testimony, silent worship and avoiding the outward observation of sacraments are the most obviously distinctive features of traditional Quakerism, though there are others. From the outside they might look like historical accidents, each with its particular justification and reason to be. However, that is not their true character. They are not held independently in a

117

rounded Quakerism, but take their strength from being integrally related to the whole.

Indeed, that is why Friends maintain them, for they are part of the reply Quakers would give to the scepticism and disorder of the modern world and the influence they would wish to exert in the church as it struggles to find its own larger response. Part of the common faith is to bear witness to one's understanding of apostolic Christianity within the fellowship. Another is to accept and learn from the diversity of witness that will arise. This can only be done if one accepts that there can be diverse insights into the common faith and that a comprehensive understanding of Christianity will be better able to meet the demands of the future than a collection of narrow sectarian ones.

It is on the issue of sacraments that these things are put to the test. Friends neither baptise with water nor observe the Lord's Supper. This mystifies many other Christians. How can that possibly be? Is not the New Testament explicit about these things? Are they not the marks of Christianity? The issue is likely to generate considerable heat; we are not dealing here with rarified heights of doctrine but with the common experiences of millions of people.

To make sense, Christianity has to speak about God. If the God question can be put in such a way that Christianity has nothing to say, its God is false and its worship meaningless. Quaker silence is therefore related intimately to an understanding of the nature of the divine. There are Friends who do not accept the Christian understanding of God, and for them the question of the sacraments is irrelevant. The majority, however, do, and it is their conception of the way God works that causes them not to baptise or celebrate the communion.

It will be generally agreed that God is the divine principle of creation and meaning. Beauty and love are expressions of the divine energy and consciousness, and we tend to use the word 'truth' to encompass everything we know about the divine. Another useful word is 'ultimate'. It indicates the limits of our understanding and powers, that beyond which we are unable to go. The word 'God' means all these things, but if it is to be taken in a Christian sense, it must additionally mean that God com-municates with us—that there is a divine revelation.

Friends believe the Bible to teach that this revelation comes directly to every single human being, without exception. Not everybody responds to revelation; we are free to ignore it or disobey it as we wish. It states, but does not compel. It can show us meaning but needs no interpretation in itself; we know inwardly that this revelation is the truth, and it guides us and lays burdens upon us when we embrace it as the source of spiritual life. It draws us into the company of others and redeems us out of the world. This is the work of the Holy Spirit, what Friends call the Light of Christ within.

We have to be careful not to confuse what is revealed and the identity of the revealer. It by no means follows from the foregoing that what God reveals to us is necessarily subjective just because we receive it within. Our manner of reception has to be intimate and personal, for we are persons, but that does not mean that there can be no public truths to which our understanding must bow. It means simply that for us to receive something as a spiritual truth, it must come to us from God alone. There are truths God teaches us directly without intermediary. There are lessons that come to us from life which God teaches us to recognise as truths. The point at which what is learned becomes truth is the point of revelation.

Friends have always seen this process of revelation as taking place continually and personally. Revelation comes to individuals, and they act upon it. Since their actions become a part of history, the course of human events reflects in a particularly vivid way the continual revelation of God and the constant human resistance to divine leadings. It seems obvious. The world is full of horror, and God is full of light. What other explanation can there be but human disobedience?

Quaker tradition has always looked on history in general, and church history in particular, as a record of the conflict between revelation and resistance. It discerns a continuing process by which those in human authority seek to utilise religion for their own purposes. Those who respond to God and live as instruments of the divine will are in the prophetic stream. Those who make religion outward and obvious, render it predictable and controllable thereby. It may not be their intention, but they open the way for it to be manipulated. Such is the priestly tradition.

The substance of history can therefore be seen as the conflict between actions taken under divine guidance and those which negligently or deliberately frustrate the divine purpose. Every part of human history will display the same features, but it is classically exemplified in the Bible. This is why, for most of their own history, the Quakers have asserted that the authority of scripture arises not because it is an inspired writing, but because it is a record of *authoritative events* which are themselves the source of revelation.

This is half the story. Friends would go on to assert that this lesson can only be learned if one sees the record with the eyes of faith. The Bible is a living document to the extent that one comes to it with the same inspiration as those who wrote it. There is no escape from the commitment of faith. Those who hear the gospel and respond to God under the leadings of the Holy Spirit will receive their revelation, for they will have taken sides in history.

This point needs labouring. Most of us do not think of history like this today. Perhaps that is part of a civilization losing its soul. We think of trends, movements, influences, disembodied processes which take place anyway, regardless of our wishes or decisions. Ultimately, we only matter as part of the mass. We are unused to the conception that history is part of God's dealings with us and that religion is the best guide to its meaning.

Very subtly the anti-prophetic tradition insulates us from all this by creating a specifically 'religious' kind of history shut up in a godly intellectual ghetto. If we can confine this sort of history to the Bible, we can distance ourselves from its demands. Religious history will be seen to happen only between the covers of a black book. The people involved in it have beards and wear funny clothes. This religious history peters out somewhere after the Acts of the Apostles. It may well be part of 'God's Plan,' but our part in the whole process is passive rather than active. It is all done for us; we are not participants.

We can be involved, however. If we are committed to Christ, as our personal saviour and as the only source of meaning and significance in life, Christ's coming into the world and his leaving of it are events of supreme importance. In all its brevity and obscurity, the Old Testament records the period of preparation for Christ's coming. The New Testament, having told his story, goes on to chart the consequences. But the fulfillment occurs in the life of each person who hears and responds to the gospel through the inward call of God. Our church membership, our prayers and our worship are all a part of that response.

So what did Christ come to do? What sort of worship did Christ institute? At this point Friends may legitimately be asked why they do not carry out Christ's clear commands. According to Matthew,

Christ told his disciples to baptise all nations. According to a tradition first recorded by Paul, Christ told his disciples at the last supper to "Do this in memory of me." What sort of Christian ignores these things?

The question is deceptively simple and cannot be directly answered, for scripture has to be taken as a whole, not as a series of disconnected proof texts. What Friends have said is that the total message of the New Testament is such that these practises are neither obligatory to Christians nor necessary to salvation—a riposte to both the Catholic and Protestant traditions in their usual forms.

Though it can be put in terms of modern critical scholarship, Friends' doctrine did not originate there, for theological liberalism is not a necessary consequence of Quaker faith, however much some Quakers think it is. The position depended originally on a pre-critical acceptance of the text of the Bible and in no sense represented an attempt to explain away uncongenial arguments on the basis that they are critically or textually unsound.

The Quaker case is by nature cumulative, and it is as important to notice what it does not say as what it does. To begin with, one cannot seriously deny that entry to the early church was by water baptism or that the eucharist soon became the main public testimony of the new community. But what *can* be asserted is that the continuation of these practises is due to historical factors, and it is possible to remain entirely true to apostolic Christianity and not do them.

Consider first the work of Christ. Undeniably the Christian must assert that Christ's reconciling work inaugurated a new dispensation in the relations between God and humanity. When pressed as to the nature of that new life, the response equally must be that it is lived under the sustaining guidance of the Holy Spirit. It is the fulfillment of our humanity.

If we then go on to ask what sort of worship will characterise this new life, the answer must be that it will be sharply distinguishable from what has gone before. Since God is a spirit, people who worship him will do so "in spirit and in truth." The distinguishing feature is not novelty but fulfillment. If many of the stories, events and practises recorded in the Old Testament are in some sense pointing towards the coming of Christ, one can expect their full significance to be revealed by him.

The biblical record bears witness to Christ's teaching as part of the fulfillment. Christ inaugurated the reign of grace to replace the rule of outward convention and replaced the regulation of the law with the intuition of the gospel. He devalued outward expression to perfect an inward integrity. As the only high priest, Christ came to do away with all ritual and to terminate the corruption of religion. What Christian will not accompany Friends at least this far?

Now consider the nature of baptism and the common meal. They are public ceremonies and they have their origin in the old dispensation. They were once part of the system of outward observances that is fundamentally inimical to the gospel. They certainly have a transformed meaning and a significance, but it is possible to doubt whether the evidence is weighty enough for us to claim it as certain that they were ordained as an observance for all time.

The eucharistic words, for example, were spoken to a specific group on a special occasion. They could apply to all meals, not just the ceremonial one. Baptism and water baptism are different things. Is it not with fire that we are to be baptised? In his first letter, Peter described baptism as the answer of a good conscience before God. Is that more or less important than dipping in water, or a matter of an entirely different order?

These may look like debating points, but they are not intended to be. If all the New Testament evidence is taken together, it is possible to see shades of opinion among the first Christians, trends of thought and, indeed, explicit differences of opinion. There is plenty of evidence that old ways of thinking continued in the church, and it is at the very least plausible that compromises were made with these ways of thinking that entrenched baptism and the supper as institutions, when a true understanding of the gospel would have required their abandonment. The fact that they continued does not prove that they were always intended to.

To back up their contention that these ceremonies were never part of the Lord's intentions for his church, Friends have always asserted the essential spiritual truths which they express. Water and washing as a symbol of a new life are so obvious as hardly to need comment. Baptism is a beginning, a turning of the heart to God, and there is no other way to enter the kingdom. But its reality is purely spiritual and therefore essentially invisible.

Likewise with the eucharist. What does Christ say in John's

Gospel? "If you do not eat the flesh of the Son of Man and drink his blood, you will not have life in you." Also, "I am the bread of life. He who comes to me will never be hungry; he who believes in me will never thirst." Of course these words can be interpreted symbolically so as to support sacramental observance in the church. But they also bear a mystical interpretation which says that they are an invitation to a direct experience, and that is essentially invisible too.

The third part of Friends' argument is a practical one and also stems from the way we understand the Bible. The struggle between the inward prophetic faith and the forces at work to corrupt the purity of religion does not end with the close of the New Testament. In the twin ceremonies of baptism and eucharist, a pair of Trojan horses were hauled into the church, for round them grew up a system of belief, practise and worship that we believe is demonstrably foreign to apostolic precedents and a spiritual understanding of scripture.

This system is commonly attributed to the adoption of Christianity by the Emperor Constantine, but his name is largely symbolic in this connection. Those, like Friends, who stand out from the mainstream of the Christian church trace back to Constantine's time a number of things they believe to be departures from the gospel. These departures can easily be explained if we view the central theme of the Bible as resistance to revelation.

When the Roman state became officially Christian, practise was placed above profession. The era of conformist Christianity began. The truth that the church and the world are in opposition was forgotten. A docile church punished its unorthodox children with great severity. It gave power into the hands of a male hierarchy and instituted a system in which grace was seen to flow only through a few rigidly controlled channels. Baptism and the eucharist as institutions—outward, easily recognisable rituals—became definitive of Christianity and thus entered that wider stream of western culture which is now in grave crisis.

The effect of most reform movement in Christianity has been to assert that rituals should not define the faith—faith should define rituals. Early Quakerism, however, was revolutionary in intent. It denied any connection at all between rituals and faith, thus making it almost impossible to draw a clear parallel between the silent meeting for worship and the holy communion, however observed. Quakerism is a radical critique of the church as an adequate vehicle for the Christian faith, not just a movement for reform. Hence the impossibility of making a straight equivalence between the silent meeting for worship and the holy communion.

Quakerism still takes this view because it has always stressed the ethical and spiritual aspects of Christianity at the expense of its doctrine and structure. Friends have made the historical judgment that the church has elevated ceremonial observance out of its place as a dying survival of the old covenant and has established ceremonial observance at the centre rather than the periphery of the faith. The church has thereby enabled itself to acquire wealth and worldly power contrary to whatever can be known of the intention of its founder.

Moreover, it follows from the Quaker view of history that while rituals exist, the danger will exist. Most Friends would disagree with a triumphalist Quakerism asserting (as it founders in effect did) that the Society of Friends is the one true church. Nevertheless, it has these questions for the rest of the body of Christians, and for its own members it should have a warning of too close an identification of the silent meeting as a eucharist without the elements.

The silent meeting has eucharistic elements to be sure, in the sense that all Christian worship is eucharistic, but not in the sense that it is always an explicit corporate memorial of the Last Supper and the death of Christ. That is less important than it sounds, though, for many other churches celebrate the communion service at infrequent intervals. What matters is the memory, not the memorial.

We must know the experience of baptism whether or not we go through the waters. We must have communion with God with or without the bread and wine. In silence Friends know these things and are not prepared to be excluded from the church because they fail, out of loving principle, to observe the practises which have claimed the loyalty of some of the greatest villains in history.

The
Common
Faith

In my third undergraduate year, the Hungarian Uprising of 1956 took place, and we had a meeting of all the students in my college to see whether there was any help we could possibly offer to the thousands of refugees who were then flooding across the Austrian frontier. About a hundred of us were present, crammed into a small room, crouching on the floor, perching on the windowsills and crowding uncomfortably round the door. A lot of ingenious, idealistic, but quite impracticable suggestions were made. We desperately wanted to help, but had no idea of where to begin.

Sitting in the middle of the floor was a slightly stout student whom, at that time, I did not know. He interrupted the discussion at one point and told us we were all starting at the wrong place, asking the wrong questions. It was simple, he told us. The naked needed warmth, the sick needed attention, and the hungry needed food. If we kept that in mind we would be able to work out what we might be able to do.

I suppose we thought he was a harmless religious crank of some sort, for in those days, people were well enough educated to recognise his allusion immediately, but far too well-bred to allow it to influence their decisions in any way. I certainly do not recall any notice being taken of what he had said. And apart from that incident, my memories of the rest of the meeting are vague.

It proved to be very important in my life, though. In my Easter vacation the year before, I had done two weeks work in my father's builders yard to earn enough money to buy a goosedown sleeping bag for when I went camping with the scouts. I had it with me on my bed in college. After the meeting, I went straight up to my room to fetch it and took it round to the shop run by the Oxford Committee for Famine Relief, as Oxfam was then known, and gave it in to the Hungarian relief appeal.

When I came out of that shop I had stepped into the kingdom, and though I would not have used these words then, I had given my life to Christ. I owed it to the witness of the short student, who afterwards became one of my dearest friends. He is a Roman Catholic. I am a convinced Quaker. We are separated by the Catholic Church, but united by the larger catholic faith—those things that have been believed everywhere, by everybody, at all times.

I am well aware that I am treading on the edge of a theological minefield to put it like that, but I am unrepentant. The Religious Society of Friends has a history of highly vocal opposition to much of what the rest of the universal church does, so I owe an explanation to both my Quaker and my Catholic friends.

In my own life there is a grey area between the common experience of the church and my own personal reflections. I have problems of belief, and I am not always at ease with the ethical guidance I receive. I am not one of those self-sufficient Friends who resist being told anything in case it interferes with their principles. Nor do I believe that orthodoxy is all—even Quaker orthodoxy. I often feel ground between two millstones. To the heretically inclined, I am suspect. To the orthodox, I am unsound.

But on the whole, I am happy with this. Nowadays, there is a tolerance between the individual and the group which has seldom been found before in Christian history. Friends tend to emphasise the intolerance of the wider church and their own religious emancipation, but that is part of a small, articulate body needing to demonstrate its own distinctiveness. The claim cannot be accepted without serious qualification.

If we went about hunting for instances of people and churches departing from respect and loving care for one another, we should not have far to go. The church, as a whole, has not been a very good advertisement for Christ. Yet if it is Christ you seek, you will find him in the church, with all its faults and human limitations. So in this inward space where I struggle with myself and with the faith, I shall need to be able to believe in the real goodness of the church as a way of becoming legitimately entitled to judge it on its shortcomings, and to discern the difference between what it claims and what it is entitled to claim.

This is an important part of my religious life, because it enables me to enter creatively into the process of forming Christian faith for my own times and contributes to that deposit of common experience which forms the tradition. It is where Christians are made, and also Christianity. The church is never going to be perfect because all our intellectual, moral and spiritual attempts to state the faith in absolute terms will be frustrated by our own imperfections. We should not look for absolutes. We should not look for perfection. We should not accept any authority that is self-authenticating. The church is imperfect because we all belong to it.

It has been my argument that there is a grey area between the common experience of the church and our own lives as individuals where we experience faith. It is in this grey area that, given a fundamental honesty, our faith is put to the test, and where we have to discern and find answers to both the legitimate and also the spurious challenges of the world. We come to new certainties as we forsake old ones, we compromise, endure and prevail.

If we can take the difficulties of these lives and out of them make a warm and heartfelt confession that our church is where we belong and want to be, we can reconcile our own integrity and the collective wisdom. That requires basic spiritual commitment from us, and a certain clarity of understanding on the part of our church.

I am not alarmed by the apparent imprecision of this formulation, for I am seeking to place the doctrinal, intellectual part of the Christian tradition in some sort of context rather than to deny it. Personally I am quite willing to be bound by the agenda it raises, though I reserve my position on things like bishops and water baptism, as all good Quakers should. In the language of the previous generation but one, I believe in truth that it is possible to discover the *essence* of Christianity and to find the essence of Quakerism within that distillation.

It is almost axiomatic to me that any systems of belief human beings can devise will tend to throw up contradictory conclusions from one set of data. Actually that is not a very original observation. But it has troublesome consequences. We find we are put to choices we would rather not make. Then there are often highly uncongenial conclusions lying embedded in the system in such a way that we cannot simply yank them out and throw them away. This is the rub. Often the kind of Christianity we loathe has brought us the Christ we love.

Certain very interesting consequences flow from this way of looking at our common faith. The first ought to be an arresting one for Quakers and Roman Catholics, who both hold variations of the doctrine that we are under the continual guidance of the Holy Spirit, collectively in our church structures as well as individually in our private lives. It is that, historically, doctrinal development comes about because the Christian system contains inherent tensions and contradictions which it perpetually seeks to resolve.

The second consequence is that the disciplines of the interior life provide an alternative method to doctrinal dispute as a way of dealing with these stresses. Secreted within the organism that is the historical Christian faith, there is a mystical and spiritual tradition which uses metaphor, symbol, image and art to come to terms with the questions thrown up by the lifestyle and religious commitment that it has made and to which it remains loyal.

It could be that the modern ecumenical movement is essentially such a quest for meaning through spirituality. Catholics wanting to take communion with Methodists, or Quakers willing to take communion with anybody, are left in no doubt that they are departing from the party line. One sometimes needs a strong conscience to practise unity against the wishes of one's denominational authorities. But hard though it is to see it sometimes, the old, hierarchical, entirely male, theological style of church leadership is weakening. The real ecumenical movement is found among people who have experienced unity, and the universal faith is found there. But this universal faith lives in a way of life, rather than a set of beliefs.

The outlines of the common faith are becoming clearer in the ecumenical experience, and they are such that you can discern them if you want Christian unity. In the first place, that which is truly Christian is the common possession of all, reflected in the denominations, but not to be appropriated by them. Each church or community has its particular gifts, but they are held in trust for all, not possessed by the minority, which each church or denomination is. The second defining characteristic of essential Christianity is that beliefs, institutions and practises so recognised as being held in common must be clearly claimed to originate in, or show continuity with the ancient church.

More importantly, if Christians possess a common heritage which no group may presume to claim solely for itself, we must all hold that gift in trust for the world and not ourselves. There can be no frontiers of pride and privilege for Christians. Humility and love are the marks of the Son of Man and those who follow him, and these imply a respect for others which is universal, for it extends to all people, whether of other faiths or of none. Hence, the common faith will be comprehensive, not exclusive. If it is to express the abundant generosity of divine grace, it will provide the widest scope for individual interests and tastes, for this will be the practical expression of the Lord's reminder that judgment is reserved for God alone.

So if we were to ask ourselves where this common faith could be found today, we could read its signs but not perhaps clearly show it. We would need to examine and receive evidence from both official and unofficial Christianity, from denominational traditions and ecumenical idealists. We would have to attempt the difficult process of discernment and separate the kernel of our faith from the husk. We would need to sift the enduring and true from the ephemeral and the false.

In this way, we should return to where we began, in the half world between our own selves and the heritage we have received, for there is no other way to come to terms with Christianity. That is why the exercise of Quaker silence is a sign of our ultimate responsibility to God. Our Lord taught us that God is to be worshipped with all our heart, soul, strength and mind, and it is here that we strive to make meaning for ourselves.

So within the community of Christians, there has always to be a continuing debate about the nature of faith and its demands on us. Among many who are not Christians there is a similar striving for understanding. That is why Quakerism has always called its message 'Truth'. The choice of this word indicates its particular genius and also its challenge.

In the Prologue to John's Gospel, Friends found the proclamation that the world is the self-expression of God—the Logos, all that is, the way things are. They knew in themselves that they were led to seek this reality at the deepest level of their lives.

Believing as historical reality that the Word was made flesh and dwelt among us and that the light which came into the world still enlightened them, they began to preach the identity of the historic and the eternal Christ and denied the primacy of historical revelation against the continuous spiritual revelation within. Friends worshipped in silence because they saw no other way to do justice to both these parts of the Christian experience, and that is perhaps their most important contribution to an understanding of the common faith.

In our day it is difficult to enter these realities, for we live in a secular culture. We are unable to make assumptions about things of religion that were previously taken for granted. That should not worry us, for we are not the first generation to face this difficulty. Very early in the history of the church, people realised that the gospel was powerless unless those to whom it was addressed comprehended its message and its challenge and were reached by its urgency.

Looking for the common faith is another way of looking for the common gospel, for consolation and hope, reassurance and meaning. The salvation we are offered in Christ is the fullness of these things. If I am to seek to witness—and we are all under this obligation—I must live and understand the gospel. What I have sought to argue about the common heritage of Christ's followers is that to witness to the world they must live in it and speak of it. The faith begins there.

For myself, the most intimate experience I have of the world is my own loneliness. It has been said that one must be at home in the desert to be safe in the marketplace. To be sure, we have to balance out our obligation to be involved in the world and our need to retire from it, but when we have done that, we still have to take the consequences. There is an inward necessity of hardship in the Christian faith which is unavoidable. It is against all reason to love the carpenter of Nazareth as the Lord of the universe. We are always at the beginning of understanding.

Then I am conscious of time. I am over half way through my life, and I have lived through a world war, the nuclear arms race, abstract impressionism, the death of God and the end of the European colonial empires. In my lifetime the world has started to press against the limits of its natural resources. I will not accept that my children have no future, so the life-urge tells me I need a sense of history, a people, ancestors and descendants. The God who comes to me in Christ gives me faith in these things and tells me that isolation is death.

No matter how much I incline my heart to God within, I need my memory and imagination to converse with God. These are both symbolic faculties, and the symbols they make are representative of the goodness of creation. As the familiar offertory prayer goes, "...of thine own have we given thee..." I need food and companions and a vision to look up for. At the deepest level of my life, there are rocks and water, sheep, a vine, the true bread, light, wind, dust, sweat, noise, thorns, a cross and an empty tomb. Christianity teaches me that the inward realm and the outward world are one.

Finally, my death is certain, but I do not regard that with fear. I am not moved to seek my own pleasure or advantage, but rather I have a sense of missed opportunity, false starts, visions of what might have been. At one and the same time, I know the possibility of perfection and that I am a sinner. Peter said, "Depart from me, Lord, for I am a sinful man." But the Lord did not. At a camp meeting they ask for forgiveness. In a monastery they ask for mercy. I ask to be healed.

So I rest my case for a spiritual Christianity as the true one. Though it is now often overlaid by the dust of subsequent controversies, this was what the first Quakers strove for and the terms in which they saw themselves. In the silent meeting they sought to discern the voice of the spirit. The first note of their original preaching was that "Christ is come to teach his people himself." The silent meeting for worship was essential to that proclamation, and in the fellowship of the Religious Society of Friends, I have come to know its truth.